SQUADRONS!

No. 65

THE 'EAGLE' SQUADRONS
- Nos 71, 121 & 133 Squadrons -

Phil H. LISTEMANN

ISBN: 978-2-494471-14-6

Copyright

© 2024 Philedition - Phil Listemann

Colour profiles: Gaetan Marie/Bravo Bravo Aviation

GLOSSARY OF TERMS

PERSONEL :

(AUS)/RAF: Australian serving in the RAF
(BEL)/RAF: Belgian serving in the RAF
(CAN)/RAF: Canadian serving in the RAF
(CZ)/RAF: Czechoslovak serving in the RAF
(NFL)/RAF: Newfoundlander serving in the RAF
(NL)/RAF: Dutch serving in the RAF
(NZ)/RAF: New Zealander serving in the RAF
(POL)/RAF: Pole serving in the RAF
(RHO)/RAF: Rhodesian serving in the RAF
(SA)/RAF: South African serving in the RAF
(US)/RAF - RCAF : American serving in the RAF or RCAF

RANKS

G/C : Group Captain
W/C : Wing Commander
S/L : Squadron Leader
F/L : Flight Lieutenant
F/O : Flying Officer
P/O : Pilot Officer
W/O : Warrant Officer
F/Sgt : Flight Sergeant
Sgt : Sergeant
Cpl : Corporal
LAC : Leading Aircraftman

OTHER

ATA: Air Transport Auxiliary
CO : Commander
DFC : Distinguished Flying Cross
DFM : Distinguished Flying Medal
DSO : Distinguished Service Order
Eva. : Evaded
ORB : Operational Record Book
OTU : Operational Training Unit
PoW : Prisoner of War
PAF: Polish Air Force
RAF : Royal Air Force
RAAF : Royal Australian Air Force
RCAF : Royal Canadian Air Force
RNZAF : Royal New Zealand Air Force
SAAF : South African Air Force
s/d: Shot down
Sqn : Squadron
† : Killed

CODENAMES - OFFENSIVE OPERATIONS - FIGHTER COMMAND

CIRCUS:
Bombers heavily escorted by fighters, the purpose being to bring enemy fighters into combat.

RAMROD:
Bombers escorted by fighters, the primary aim being to destroy a target.

RANGER:
Large formation freelance intrusion over enemy territory with aim of wearing down enemy figthers.

RHUBARD:
Freelance fighter sortie against targets of opportunity.

ROADSTEAD:
Dive bombing and low level attacks on enemy ships at sea or in harbour

RODEO:
A fighter sweep without bombers.

SWEEP:
An offensive flight by fighters designed to draw up and clear the enemy from the sky.

Recruting American Pilots

From the very beginning of the war in Europe, Americans, at all levels, took an interest in the conflict realising that, sooner or later, they would be involved. Creating a fighter squadron comprising American volunteers quickly took root in certain minds, including Charles Sweeny's, an ex-serviceman of the French Foreign Legion during the Great War. He had been inspired by the exploits of the famous American-manned Lafayette squadron, and the status it held, all of which had been portrayed by the media of the time. He established a network, allowing interested Americans to cross the Atlantic to support France, although French enthusiasm on this occasion was not so positive. Compounding Sweeny's problems was a Congress Neutrality Act, voted in 1935 and revised and reinforced many times thereafter, making the recruiting of American volunteers for fighting in foreign countries very difficult indeed. The US authorities closely monitored activity of this nature and would not facilitate any enlistment. Volunteers or, for that matter, anyone suspected of being one, would be detained at the Canadian border. This situation remained right up until the fall of France in June 1940. As a result, volunteers arrived too late and the French, overwhelmed by their own situation, had little to offer them. Consequently, the vast majority disappeared amid the upheaval, either killed or made prisoners, while others returned to the USA by their own means. Only five of the original volunteers are known to have arrived in Great Britain.

Thereafter the situation changed and American authorities became more accommodating. At the same time the number of volunteers increased, since many were aware that the USA was preparing to enter the war. The Knight Committee, named for its founder, was set up and this organisation would be responsible for the bulk of American recruitment from the spring of 1940. In August 1941 this committee became the Canadian Aviation Bureau before it was disbanded in late 1942. Some 250 American pilots would serve with three American fighter units - the Eagle Squadrons - formed within the RAF between 1940 and 1942. These men, though, were only a fraction of the hundreds who passed through the committee to enrol in the RAF, or the RCAF, and fight under the RAF umbrella in Europe, the Middle East and the Far East. Their motives were varied, but the majority simply sought adventure. Their aspirations were to become pilots, but many had been refused entry into their own country's air arms on educational, competency or medical grounds (or a combination of those). Both the RCAF and the RAF (Royal Air Force Volunteer Reserve - RAFVR) provided viable alternatives and the prospect of flying a Spitfire, by then the best Allied fighter, only strengthened their desire to join up. The American pilots, in particular those that served with the Eagle Squadrons, were to benefit from certain privileges. Most were not required to pledge allegiance to the King upon their engagement and thus were able to maintain their American citizenship. Additionally, it was understood that, those passed by the Knight Committee would be commissioned at the end of their training, as opposed to the majority of those who joined the RCAF and graduated as Non-Commissioned Officers. This disparity was to create problems when the integration of these pilots into the USAAF took place.

The man who started it all, Colonel Sweeny, right, in RAF uniform. He served with the French Foreign Legion in early W.W.I and soon found himself in charge of its small American unit. In 1915 he was commissioned in the Legion, the first American to be so promoted. He was wounded the same year and was also the first American to be awarded the Legion of Honour. When the USA entered the war, he joined the US Army and ended the war as a lieutenant-colonel. He continued his career as a soldier of fortune post- war and, logically, when France was at war once more in 1939, he wished to help build a new Lafayette *escadrille*. France collapsed before the project came to fruition, but the RAF would inherit the project.

The end of an era. The three RAF fighter squadrons are transferred to the USAAF in a ceremony on 29 September 1942. Here Air Chief Marshal Sir Sholto Douglas, Commander-in-Chief RAF Fighter Command, is reviewing the Eagle pilots. The three Eagle squadrons had been brought together on the same base a short time earlier, having fought separately since their respective formations. Note the pilots are wearing their RAF uniforms, but all already been officially transferred to the USAAF and were no longer members of the RAF.

TRANSFER TO THE AAF

The transfer of personnel to the AAF, a natural outcome, was not so simple for numerous reasons. Firstly, the RAF had put a considerable investment into their training, and they were fully operational, and doing a fine job, when America entered the war in December 1941. The British simply were not in a hurry to disband the three American fighter squadrons. The pilots themselves had signed up with the RAFVR until the end of the war and, adding to English woes, they now faced war on a new front with Japan. Integration into the AAF meant that the pilots trained by the RAF would, sooner or later, come into contact with countrymen trained in American schools and this would not be to everyone's satisfaction. At certain levels 'Eagle' flyers had been subjected to a British influence, not always well embraced by Americans.

Rank equivalence also posed problems. The AAF did not have anyone below the base rank of second lieutenant as a pilot . NCOs transferring from the RCAF would automatically have to become second lieutenants. The situation involving officers was relatively straightforward - they would transfer to the comparative rank. There was also debate about how these transferees should be utilised. Eighth Air Force officials of rank felt that it would be logical to divide these pilots among AAF units arriving in England where their solid experience would be of some benefit.

Others were of the opinion that the three Eagle squadrons, having established a fine reputation and not wishing to separate, should be forged into a specific unit - the 4th Fighter Group (FG). In effect this was what happened in September 1942. However, some pilots chose to remain with the RAF out of loyalty and feeling a transfer would not be in their best interests. But the record was good however with over 100 enemy aircraft destroyed or probably destroyed in 11,000 operational sorties.

As for the 4th FG, it was to keep its unique identity for the early months of its existence, but, by the summer of 1943, due to losses and turnover, it would become an American Fighter Group, falling in line with all of the others. For those who chose to integrate into the AAF, it was not immediately apparent whether they had made the correct choice or not. While they gained a pay increase and access to an array of typically American luxuries, they lost an element of prestige with the British population who held them in high regard - they were considered to be a cut above the average American. There was also the loss of spirit and friendship, very present within the British units, which became more obvious with the arrival of American pilots coming from the USA to replace those who were lost or had left.

The pilots of the Eagle Squadrons were special, being volunteers in a British war that was not theirs and, for political reasons, they had been courted by and received a great deal of press. Once integration into the AAF had taken place, this became something of a burden. The AAF moved quickly to tone down their amount of press coverage, so that they would become less conspicuous, for both morale and political reasons.

Victories - confirmed or probable claims: 53.5

First operational sortie:
05.02.41
Last operational sortie:
27.09.42

Number of sorties: *ca.* 5,850

Total aircraft written-off: 38

Aircraft lost on operations: 28
Aircraft lost in accidents: 10

Squadron code letters:
XR

COMMANDING OFFICERS

S/L Walter M. Churchill	AAF No. 90241	AAF	29.09.40	23.01.41
S/L William E.G. Taylor	RAF No. 86597	(US)/RAF	23.01.41	05.06.41
S/L Henry de C.A. Woodhouse	RAF No. 34189	RAF	05.06.41	13.08.41
S/L Ernest R. Bitmead	RAF No. 34139	RAF	13.08.41	22.08.41
S/L Stanley T. Meares (†)	RAF No. 37683	RAF	22.08.41	15.11.41
S/L Chesley G. Peterson	RAF No. 83706	(US)/RAF	17.11.41	27.08.42
S/L Gregory A. Daymond	RAF No. 84657	(US)/RAF	27.08.42	29.09.42

SQUADRON USAGE

Activated on 27 March 1917, No. 71 Squadron at first mainly comprised Australian personnel serving with the Royal Flying Corps. It left for France in December with its Sopwith Camels. The unit was finally renamed No. 4 Squadron, Australian Flying Corps, on 19 January 1918. Number 71 Squadron was not 're-born' until the Second World War when American volunteers in the RAF were brought together as a unit.

While the USA did not immediately get involved in both conflicts, resourceful Americans, seeking adventure, wanting to fight against tyranny or anticipating the eventual entry of their country into the war, signed up to fight. During the First World War, an American-manned fighter squadron, the *Escadrille Lafayette*, had been activated in France to fly with the *Aéronautique Militaire*. It was named after a French hero of the American War of Independence.

As early as the beginning of WW2, American volunteers rushed toward the recruiting offices to fight in Europe. Canada was the main entry because of its proximity, but some tried their chances via other channels to join French units. While some would set foot on the Continent, none would be trained by the French; many ended up in Great Britain. The first trained American volunteers were transferred to different units of the RAF; a few even participated in the Battle of Britain, some paying with their lives. Faced with an increased influx of American volunteers, grouping them together as a fighter unit was envisaged. The idea was accepted as early as 2 July 1940. This was a time when the RAF activated many units comprising volunteers from the occupied European countries. It was important for Britain to show the rest of the world they were not the only ones willing to fight. Three fighter units, principally comprising American citizens, would be created and came to be known as the Eagle Squadrons. Only the pilots who served with one or more of the three fighter units, between 1940 and 1942, could be designated as Eagles; Americans serving with other units of the RAF or RCAF could not. It was the same for the pilots coming from the American fighter schools, who would later form the 4th Fighter Group (FG), and who in fact had nothing to do with the RAF or the RCAF, even though this unit was the direct descendant of the three Eagle Squadrons. To distinguish themselves from Americans in the RAF and RCAF who simply wore a 'USA' shoulder flash, the Eagle pilots had a special badge made.

After the Battle of Britain, 71 Squadron reformed at Church Fenton. The three Eagle Squadrons were to receive a number in the RAF's regular sequence, not what was normally reserved for squadrons consisting of mainly non-British pilots (the 300 series, for

Twelve of the first American pilots to serve with the squadron, in late April 1941. Left to right:
Charles E. Bateman from Massachusetts, William H. Nichols from California (PoW 07.09.41), Stanley M. Kolendorski from New Jersey (†17.05.41), William EG Taylor (CO) from Kansas, Andrew B. Mamedoff from Connecticut (†08.10.41 with 133 Sqn), Eugene Q. Tobin from Utah (†07.09.41), Newton Anderson from Louisiana (†29.06.42 as CO of 222 Sqn, the first American to lead an all-British fighter squadron), Luke E. Allen from Colorado, Ken S. Taylor from Manitoba, Canada (†08.08.41), Victor R. Bono born in Norway, Gregory A. Daymond from Montana, and Sam A. Mauriello from New York. All the Eagle pilots who passed through the Knight Committee received a commission upfront. All of the surviving pilots transferred to the USAAF, but Allen resigned his RAF commission later that spring, apparently for personal reasons. Bono, more obscurely, was dismissed from RAF service in March 1942. Note the first name 'Maud' painted under the cockpit.

example) as the ground personnel would be mostly British and would remain so during the units' period of existence. From the first day of 71 Squadron's service, three pilots, already serving elsewhere with operational units, were transferred in. They were Pilot Officers E. Tobin, AB Mamedoff and V. Keough. Command of the squadron was given to a British pilot, S/L W.M. Churchill, who assumed the role on 29 September, while the flight commander positions were filled a month later, again by British pilots (Flight Lieutenants G.A. Brown and R.C. Wilkinson). For the Americans, this situation was not at first looked upon favourably as they wanted a 100% American unit under the command of the RAF, nothing less. The formation of 71 was highly publicised by the British who needed to show that Americans were already fighting at their side. For these purposes, no British pilots were present in the photographs released to the media. It was a big disappointment, especially for William Taylor, an ex-USN pilot, who had expected to command the squadron but instead became Churchill's deputy. The reality for the RAF, however, having already commissioned several similar squadrons, was that the 'newcomers' needed to gain experience, not just in action against the Luftwaffe, but in the way the RAF did things. It, therefore, had been agreed that leadership roles would be filled by Americans once this requisite experience had been acquired. Meanwhile, the pilots slowly arrived but training was not homogenous (71 Squadron comprised several relatively experienced flyers as already mentioned), as the vast majority of assigned pilots were fresh from schools and needed to complete their training. The squadron eventually attained its normal quota of pilots towards the end of November. Meanwhile, on 8 October 1940, the British officially announced the existence of No. 71 (Eagle) Squadron. Regarding the aircraft, the first arrived on 24 October; they were three Brewster Buffaloes, recovered from a Belgian contract. The choice of this small fighter was odd, but may have been an attempt to get the Americans flying with something 'familiar'. The Brewsters were quickly judged unfit for combat by S/L Churchill himself who opposed the sending of additional machines. One of the aircraft was damaged by P/O Leckrone on 28 October, when he overturned during landing. At the same time, Churchill managed to obtain a quick replacement and, on 7 November, 71 took charge of its first nine Hurricane Mk.Is. They were far from new aircraft and the majority had seen combat during the preceding weeks so were a bit weary. They were certainly better than the Buffaloes, though, which left the squadron on 10 November. To complete its training, the unit left for Kirton in Lindsey, a base that would be used until April 1941. Despite unfa-

Walter Churchill joined the Auxiliary Air Force in 1931 and commissioned with No. 605 (County of Warwick) Squadron in 1932. In 1937 he went on to the Reserve of Officers and was recalled to full-time service with the squadron in August 1939. In November he was posted to No. 3 Squadron as a flight commander and followed the unit to France in May 1940. He made his first, and only, claims during the Battle of France and returned to Britain with six confirmed victories (two being shared) and two inconclusive (the term 'probable' would be used later). When the CO was killed in action on 16 May, he took command of the squadron. By the end of May the squadron was withdrawn to Kenley and Churchill had been awarded both the DSO and the DFC. In June he was posted to his former unit as OC and participated in the Battle of Britain. At the end of September he left 605 to become the first OC of No. 71 (Eagle) Squadron the first fighter unit to be manned by American pilots. However, due to a recurrent sinus problem, he had to relinquish his command in January 1941 and remained grounded for a period. Fit again for operational flying, he was posted overseas as a Group Captain, in July 1942, to command RAF Takali in Malta where furious combats were engaged. He flew a Spitfire off the aircraft carrier HMS *Furious* on 11 August 1942 and landed on Malta. He planned the first offensive sweeps over Sicily on the 23rd and, four days later while leading the second one, his Spitfire crashed in flames after being hit by flak. There was no chance of survival for Churchill.

Hawker Hurricane Mk I v7608
No. 71 (Eagle) Squadron
Kirton-in-Lindsey (UK), winter 1940-1941

This page and next. Like many squadrons, 71 began working up on war-weary Hurricane Mk.Is. By the spring of 1941, these were replaced by brand-new Hurricane Mk.IIs, which had better performance. The Hurricanes are wearing post-Battle of Britain camouflage and markings, most of the time masking the serials. However, 'XR-J' above was V7608 and (next page) 'XR-F' was V7319.

Among the founding members of the squadron were three Battle of Britain veterans: Eugene Q. Tobin from Utah, Vernon C. Keough from New Jersey, and Andrew B. Mamedoff from Connecticut. All had previously flown with 609 Sqn and were posted together to the newly formed Eagle squadron. The latter is proudly displaying the badge adopted by all the American pilots posted to the Eagle squadrons. All three were killed during 1941, Tobin and Keough with 71 Sqn and Mamedoff with 133 Sqn.

vourable weather, training continued to bring the squadron up to an operational standard. This would not be without incident, however, as after the engine failure suffered by P/O V. Keough on the first day of the 1941, necessitating an emergency landing near the station, Pilot Officers P. Leckrone and E. Orbison collided in mid-air five days later. While Orbison manage to return to Kirton in Lindsey, Leckrone was left with no option but to abandon his out-of-control Hurricane. For unknown reasons, he was unable to do so and was killed in the subsequent crash. Leckrone was one of the seven American pilots to have participated in the Battle of Britain and his experience was of great value to the unit at this early stage. At the end of the month, Churchill had to leave for medical reasons and was temporarily replaced by S/L W. Taylor. During his command, Taylor instilled in his pilots an impeccable discipline which, while not always appreciated, would be helpful in the following weeks. The squadron was finally declared operational at the end of January 1941.

On 5 February, 71 Squadron carried out its first sortie, a patrol by Pilot Officers C.G. Peterson and L. Allen between 13.18 and 14.20. Local patrols comprised all of the squadron's early operational sorties, easing the unit in as it were. At the time, while the squadron had been declared operational, not all its pilots were regarded similarly. Early in the month one, P/O K.F. Kennerly, was even sent back to the USA due to his unsuitability. Operational flying may have started quietly, but two pilots were killed within a few weeks. Pilot Officer Orbison, having survived the mid-air collision with the now late Leckrone, ran out of luck on the 9th when he lost control of his aircraft during a patrol. Six days later, P/O V.C. Keough, another Battle of Britain veteran (No. 609 Squadron), was seen to crash into the water at great speed during a sortie over the North Sea. It was later discovered he had apparently not turned his oxygen on properly and lost consciousness as a result. Fifty-two sorties were carried out in February, followed by ninety more in March, but still combat claims eluded the Americans. The disappointing results were such that sending the pilots home, if things didn't improve in the weeks to come, was considered an option. In the hope of making things more favourable, 71 Squadron was transferred to the south-east of England on 9 April, coming under the command of No. 11 Group at Martlesham Heath, where encounters with the Luftwaffe were more likely. This change seemed to bear fruit as early as 13 April when the first German aircraft was encountered; the Ju88 escaped into cloud. The number of sorties increased to 190 in April, still without results. Worse, another loss was suffered when P/O J.L. McGinnis was killed on take-off for a patrol on 26 April. During the last days of April, 71 began to

The first American pilot to be killed in action against the Luftwaffe was P/O 'Mike' Kolendorski. From New Jersey, he was proud of his Polish roots and displayed the Polish Air Force national markings on his flying suit. He's seen here jumping into a Hurricane for the camera. Note the aircraft is wearing the Eagle squadron badge painted under the exhaust pipes; this was not a very common practice.

exchange its ageing Hurricane Mk.Is for Mk.IIs; the first sorties on the new aircraft were carried out on the 20th. By the end of April, all of the old machines were gone. May was the month of major changes. On the 9th, B Flight saw a change of command as P/O C.G. Peterson, an American, took over. A few days later, 71 finally opened its score. On the 15th, ten Hurricanes scrambled from Martlesham Heath at 20.30. They were soon ordered to patrol Canterbury at 20,000 feet. When over the city, they were vectored 150° for eight minutes and then told to orbit. They were flying over Calais in sections of two at 22,000 feet when Bf109s were spotted 2,000 feet below. Red Section, led by F/L G.A. Brown, dived after the enemy aircraft but could not catch up, rejoining the rest of the squadron at 21,000 feet. Yellow Section, led by P/O J.K .Alexander, which had followed Red Section down, continued the chase and Alexander was able to fire a two-second burst from 500 yards astern at a Bf109 without effect; the pursuit, however, had put Yellow Section in a very bad position as they were soon attacked by other Bf109s. Fortunately, the rest of the squadron joined them and a furious dogfight ensued. Alexander again managed to fire a long burst at another Bf109 from astern, this time closing to 150 yards. He saw his fire enter the Bf109 which climbed steeply for 500 feet, pouring black smoke, and suddenly nosed over into an uncontrolled spin towards the sea from 10,000 feet. Alexander did not see the Bf109 crash as he was obliged to assist his wingman, P/O J. Flynn, who had been attacked and badly damaged; the offending Bf109 had, in the meantime, abandoned the attack when he saw the English coast, but Flynn needed assistance to make his way back so was escorted by Alexander to Manston where he crash landed. Pilot Officer Alexander went on to claim a Bf109 probably destroyed. The Germans got their revenge two days later by shooting down P/O S. Kolendorski, when, while patrolling with nine others, he decided to chase a Bf109 and broke formation without orders, possibly falling into a trap. He was the first Eagle pilot to be killed in action. Despite this loss, May was seen as a positive; the Americans were happy to be in the thick of the action and flew more than 450 sorties for the month.

In June, Taylor was replaced by a British pilot, S/L Woodhouse, but, despite close to 600 sorties being flown, the month was otherwise uneventful. On the 23rd, 71 moved to North Weald. On 2 July, the squadron flew its first offensive mission by escorting Blenheims to Lille where they were tasked to bomb a power station. The formation was intercepted by 24 Bf109s after reaching the town and in the ensuing melee three were claimed as destroyed (the CO, and Pilot Officers W.R. Dunn and G.A. Daymond), one probably destroyed (P/O R.L. Mannix) and one damaged (P/O V.R. Bono). Pilot Officer W.I. Hall, however, was lost to the Bf109s. He was seen to drop out of the fight with smoke pouring from his aircraft but was later reported as a PoW. Two days later, P/O K.S. Taylor added a Bf109, damaged near Bethune, to 71's scoreboard and, on the 6th, near Lille, Daymond added another Bf109 confirmed, while F/L C.G .Peterson claimed a Bf109 probably destroyed and Dunn shared one with a Polish pilot from No. 306 Squadron. The squadron continued its success two weeks later when Bono claimed a Bf109 probably destroyed west of Lille on the 19th and

William Erwin Gibson TAYLOR
RAF No. 85597

William Taylor had served as a pilot with the United States Marine Corps when he decided to join the Royal Navy (RN) in 1939. After a refresher train-ing course, he became a carrier-qualified pilot and participated in the Norwegian campaign aboard HMS Glorious. On return from the campaign, he was sent to the USA as part of the British Purchasing Commission attempting to obtain new aircraft for the RN. There, he decided to join the Clayton Knight Committee instead, which was recruiting American pilots for the RAF. Therefore, owing to his experience and rank, he resigned his RN commission and enlisted in the RAF in October 1940 when the first Eagle Squadron, No. 71, was formed under a British CO. He helped the new squadron reach operational status and was even-tually posted to command in January 1941. He left in June, resigning his commission, and returned to the USA where he enlisted in the USN Reserve as a lieutenant commander. He served for the remainder of the war, and beyond, with the USN, eventually resigning for good in 1951.

Hawker Hurricane Mk. I Vxxx7
No. 71 (Eagle) Squadron
Martlesham Heath (UK), spring 1941

Dunn claimed another destroyed over the same place two days later. At the end of July, P/O A.B. Mamedoff became A Flight CO opposite F/L R.C. Wilkinson; now 71 had two American flight commanders. In August, the first Eagle Squadron continued its run of success. On the 3rd, while on a convoy patrol off Orfordness, Daymond caught a marauding Do17. Closing in, he opened fire from about 250 yards with a three-second burst; the rear gunner returned fire but ceased after the second burst fired by Daymond who continued his attack, firing his remaining ammunition. The Dornier hit the water and bounced off, before settling and sinking immediately. Sadly, two days later, P/O W.R. Driver was killed heading out for a sweep; he was seen in a dive, for unknown reasons, a mile north of Middle Waltham. The winds of change had begun to blow when the first Spitfire Mk.IIs arrived. The Hurricanes continued to be used, however, and the last claims were made on 19 August, coinciding with the last sorties performed on the type. While providing an escort to Blenheims for *Circus* 82, 71 was intercepted by Bf109s off Gravelines. Two claims were made: P/O M.W. Fessler for one Bf109 probably destroyed, while another was damaged by P/O H.S. Fenlaw. It wasn't a one-sided encounter, though, as P/O V.W. Olson was apparently hit by flak. Rather than bale out over France to become a prisoner, Olson elected to take his chances and nurse his stricken aircraft out over the North Sea where he baled out. Although his parachute was seen to open properly, he was never found. His body was eventually recovered on the Dutch coast. The next day, the squadron took off in the Spitfire Mk.IIs, closing the Hurricane era which had seen over 2,325 sorties flown (all but 320 on the Mk.IIs).

The first Spitfire Mk.IIs were taken on charge between 6 and 12 August 1941 (P7430, P7610, P7738, P7776, P7818, P7987, P8033/T, P8080, P8169, P8375, P8396, P8423/S, P8436 and P8702). The squadron was still commanded by a British pilot, S/L H. de C.A. Woodhouse, but he was soon replaced by another British officer, S/L E.R. Bitmead, who, in turn, led for just a week before having to relinquish command due to poor health. He was replaced by S/L S.T. Meares from the 22nd. Conversion was quick, but it came at a cost with the death of P/O K.S. Taylor on the 8th during a practice flight. He hit the ground while recovering from a dive and was killed instantly. Taylor was born in Canada, but at least one of his parents was American. The first operational sorties, some convoy patrols, were flown on the 17th. Even the Hurricanes continued to fly operationally for the next two days. On the evening of the 20th, 71 participated in the first sweep with its first aircraft (led by F/L Mamedoff). That was followed the next day by two bom-

Hurricane Mk.IIs of 71 Sqn at dispersal at Martlesham Heath during the summer of 1941. Some aircraft appear ready for an immediate take-off, as seen by the parachutes on the stabilisers.

ber escorts, one in the morning and one in the afternoon, both led by Mamedoff. All were uneventful if we exclude some aircraft returning early due to engine trouble. After a couple of days of reduced operational activity, 71 returned over the continent on the 25th with the new CO in the lead, but returned with nothing to report. That day, the first Rhubarbs were also flown. On the 27th, 71 participated in Circus 86, an escort for nine Blenheims to Lille. On the return journey, the squadron was flying at 17,000 feet when P/O W.R. Dunn developed oxygen trouble. He had to descend to 8000 feet as a result and flew below the bombers. At about five miles from the French coast a Bf109 attacked him from above and behind, but slightly overshot Dunn in the dive. Dunn raised the nose of his Spitfire and gave him a three second burst from 100 yards. Black and white smoke poured from the engine and the pilot baled out at about 7000 feet. Immediately after, another Bf109 made a similar attack, but it turned to the right to disengage. Dunn followed, managed to get in a good position, and gave a 4.5 second burst from 200 to 50 yards. The Bf109 burst into flames and crashed. This was not the end of the combat, however, as a third Bf109 appeared and was more accurate than its predecessors as its cannon fire struck Dunn's aircraft behind the cockpit rendering the R/T unserviceable and wounding his right foot in the process. The Bf109 continued its pursuit, but could not hit the Spitfire again. It eventually veered off and left the area. Dunn returned to base where he landed his damaged aircraft safely. He was off duty for a couple of weeks. Dunn's achievement was the first double claim made by a 71 Squadron pilot and would be the only ones made while flying the Spitfire Mk.II despite the rest of the month remaining busy. The squadron flew every day, carrying out eighty sorties during convoy patrols, Rhubarbs and bomber (29th) and destroyer escorts (31st). In the final days of August, the first Spitfire Mk.V arrived at the squadron. Indeed, 71 introduced the Mk.V on 1 September, but flew both types until mid-month. Two major operations, Circus ops, on the 1st and the 4th took care of the final combat work for the Spitfire IIs. After that date, the squadron flew the Mk.V. In all, 71 flew less than 250 sorties with the Spitfire Mk.II.

The first Spitfire Vs (W3509, W3627, AB783, AB810-11, AB875, AB900, AB907, AB815 and AD123) arrived just before the end of August and the first operations were flown alongside Spitfire IIs. There was no need to waste time converting to the Mk.V as the two types were very similar. The full complement of Spitfire Vs had been received by early September and it cannot be said that the introduction of the Mk.V did not get off to a good start for the squadron. While only two confirmed victories had been claimed with the Spitfire IIs in over a month, the unit claimed two Bf109s destroyed, another probable and one damaged during a bomber escort to Mazingarbe on the 4th. The victorious pilots were P/O G.A. Daymond from Montana, P/O T.C. Wallace from Pennsylvania, P/O R.L. Mannix from New York, and P/O M.W. Fessler from Wisconsin. Those claims were made for no loss so it really was a good start. Three days later, the squadron, led by the CO, took part in a sweep to St-Omer in the north of France. The Luftwaffe did not make it easy for them. While F/L Chesley Peterson, the American B Flight commander from Idaho, managed to shoot down a Bf109, the engagement was not one-sided and three pilots were posted missing. Pilot Officers H.S. Fenlow from Texas and E.Q. Tobin from Utah were both later declared killed in action. Eugene Tobin was a great loss for the squadron as he was a founding member of the

The Spitfire Mk.II, P7308/XR-D, in which William R. Dunn claimed two victories - the sole occasion a Mk.II of 71 Sqn was flown with success. Damage to the tail is clearly visible and Dunn was wounded during the combat, which resulted in him being repatriated.

Stanley Thomas MEARES
RAF No. 37683

Stanley Meares joined the RAF on a short service commission in January 1936. Upon his training being completed in January 1937, he was posted to No. 74 Squadron, the unit he was still serving with when war broke out. Late in 1939, he was posted to HQ Fighter Command and would not return to an operational unit until May 1941 when he was posted to No. 611 (County of Lancashire) Squadron as a flight commander. On the 28th he made his first claim, a Bf109 destroyed, followed by another on 22 June, and one damaged on 30 June. The same day, he was posted back to his first unit, No. 74 Squadron, to take command. In July he made two more claims, Bf109s damaged on the 4th and the 5th. A DFC followed two weeks later. In August he was posted to No. 71 (Eagle) Squadron as OC and shot down a Bf109, his last claim, on 2 October. He commanded the squadron until he was killed during a practice flight on 15 November 1941.

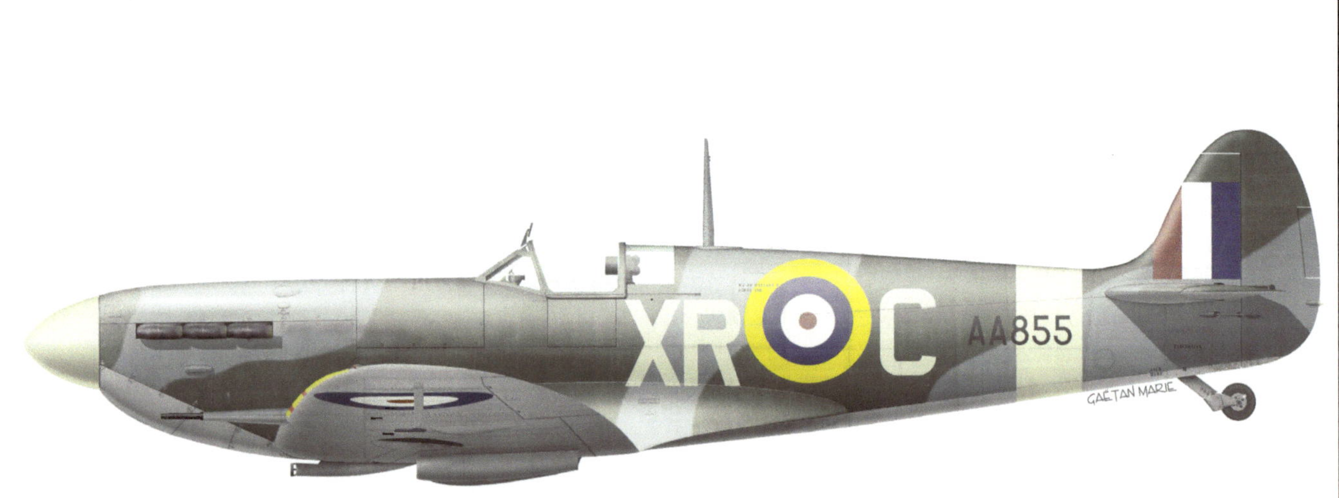

Supermarine Spitfire Mk VB AA855
No. 71 (Eagle) Squadron
North Weald (UK), autumn 1941

Two prominent American faces of 71 Sqn during the Spitfire era. Left, 'Gus' Daymond and, right, 'Pete' Peterson. The photo was taken when both were awarded the DFC, the first Eagles to receive the award. At the time, Peterson was a flight commander and was to become the only Eagle pilot to receive the DSO when he was awarded it in September 1942.

unit and had fought in the Battle of Britain with No. 609 Squadron. The third pilot missing, P/O W.H. Nichols from California, was captured and was sent to a PoW camp. A fourth Spitfire, flown by Texan P/O F.P. Dowling, was seriously damaged by the Bf109s and had to make a forced landing near the airfield. While Dowling escaped injury, his aircraft was only good for scrap. Over the next few days, 71 was involved in convoy or dawn patrols until the 16th when another sweep over France was carried out. It proved uneventful, but was followed by an escort of 24 Blenheims attacking Mazingarbe the next day (*Circus* 95). The Bf109s soon interfered over Dunkirk and Pilot Officers T.P. McGerty (Texas) and New Yorker W.D. Geiger were soon separated from the rest of the formation. McGerty was shot down and killed by the Bf109s and Geiger, with three Bf109s after him, barely avoided the same fate. Hit, he was able to bale out and land in the English Channel. After floating for about five hours, he was rescued by a German patrol boat and spent the rest of the war in captivity. Despite these two losses, another bomber escort was organised later in the evening, but this time everyone made it back to base. The squadron would get its revenge the following day when F/L Peterson claimed a Bf109 destroyed and another damaged south of Le Touquet during the first op of the day (another bomber escort). The following day, P/O G.A. Daymond, accompanied by J. Flynn from Illinois, flew a *Rhubarb* over the Continent. They encountered some Bf109s and fared well with the American pilots returning with one confirmed Bf109 each, Daymond damaging another. The second op, a naval escort, was uneventful. Bomber escort was the task given to the Wing on the 20th, the 21st and then again on the 27th. On the second of those, the Americans fought against the Bf109s once more and some pilots returned victorious. 'Red' McColpin, from New York State and recently posted from No. 121 Squadron, was successful, while P/O C.W. Tribken, also from New York State, claimed a probable. It was during the operation of the 27th (*Circus* 103), however, that the unit would make its best claims with two Bf109s destroyed, three more claimed as probables, and one damaged. The claims were shared between F/L Peterson, P/O Sam Mauriello (New York City), who opened his score after nine months of operations with the squadron, Californian P/O J.G. DuFour (but using the identity of J.J. Crowley) and R.O. Scarborough from New Mexico. Scarborough was a newcomer from No. 133 Squadron and, like DuFour and Mauriello, opened his score during this op. The damaged aircraft was claimed by O.H. Coen from North Dakota. September ended with an uneventful *Rhubarb*. The month had been a very successful and intensive one, despite the relatively small number of operations flown, 200 for the Spitfire V, compared to more than 400 in August. The introduction of the Mk.V, despite the early losses, showed promise for the squadron.

While September can be regarded as an intense month of operations, October, despite the 250 sorties flown, was almost routine. An uneventful fighter sweep was flown on the first day of the month to kick things off. The next day, 71 participated in a bomber escort to Abbeville. Intercepted by Bf109s, the squadron managed to shoot down five of them, including one for the CO, in the ensuing melee. The other four were credited to American pilots. McColpin, who was to become one of the unit's most successful pilots, shot down two, while P/O Scarborough shared a claim with P/O N. Anderson from Louisiana who opened his score in this occasion. The other claim went to another pilot who also opened his score – 'Art' Roscoe from Illinois. This tally was obtained for no loss. The following day, a bomber escort to Nieuport and a *Rhubarb* with three aircraft were flown, but no enemy aircraft were encountered. During the next six days there was no operational flying, but F/L Chesley Peterson and F/O 'Gus' Daymond were awarded the DFC on the 4th. They were the first Eagle pilots to receive this honour. On the 10th and 11th, operational flying resumed quietly with four Spitfires flying a *Rhubarb* each day and a handful of convoy patrols being dutifully carried out. On 12 October, among other operational sorties, the squadron participated in a bomber escort to Boulogne, followed by another one the next day to Mazingarbe. Twelve aircraft took off at 13.25 with the CO leading. The Luftwaffe soon made its appearance. At the end of the combat, P/O G.C. Daniel (RCAF) was missing. He was later reported as a PoW at Stalag Luft III, having drifted in his dinghy for more than seventy hours before being washed up on the shores of France suffering a fractured knee and frostbite. He was an interesting man as he was a Native American from Oklahoma and had previously served with Nos. 121 (Eagle) and 133 (Eagle) Squadrons before being posted to 71 in September. He was to be one of the few pilots to serve in all three of the Eagle squadrons. It was a period of bad luck for 71 Squadron as, two days later, Texan P/O R.A. Atkinson was killed. While doing aerobatics, a wing collapsed in level flight. Even though he baled out of his stricken aircraft, he was too low for his parachute to deploy properly and was killed when he hit the ground. Having arrived the previous month, he was about to be declared operational. One week later, the squadron lost another pilot in an accident. Pilot Officer L.A. Chatterton, from Brooklyn, also lost a wing while turning steeply. He had only begun his operational experience earlier in the month. In the meantime, operations continued and, on the 16th, the squadron was able to avenge the loss of Daniel, shot down three days previously, when, during a *Rhubarb*, McColpin managed to shoot down a Hs126. Four days later, P/O Coen took off at 06.30 with F/L 'Pete' Peterson on a *Rhubarb*. They found a train and strafed it, but Coen's Spitfire was damaged, when the train exploded, and he had to bale out. Luckily, he was not captured and, with the help of the French underground, he evaded capture and was back with the squadron at the end of December. Pilot Officer M.W. Fessler of Wisconsin had a similar experience when his Spitfire was also damaged by an exploding train on the 27th. He was not as lucky as Coen, however, and saw out the war as a PoW. On the credit side, P/O Scarborough claimed a Bf109 on the 25th while on a *Rhubarb* and McColpin made a double claim on the 27th, which took him to ace status, during the same op when Fessler was shot down.

In November, the squadron flew more than 200 sorties, a good figure considering the unit could not fly for almost half of the month. The main reason was the weather which began to deteriorate as the month progressed. Most of the sorties carried out were convoy patrols with only a handful of ops flown over the Continent. On the 1st, the squadron participated in an escort of Hurricanes and bombers to Hardelot, an op that was repeated on the 4th. Three days later, a *Rhubarb*, led by the CO, was flown during which P/O

The third Eagle pilot to receive the DFC was 'Red' McColpin, seen here congratulated by his squadron mates in November 1941 in front of his Spitfire (AB908/XR-Y) with four swastikas painted under the cockpit. McColpin also served with Nos. 121 and 133 Sqns, making him one of the very few American pilots to have served with all three of the Eagle units.

The most claims made by 71 Sqn were made while operating the Spitfire V. However, it also suffered most of its losses, including AA855/XR-C in which P/O M.W. Fessler was shot down to become a PoW on 27 October 1941. *(Andrew Thomas)*

T.C. Wallace (Pennsylvania) claimed a Bf109 destroyed over the Dunkirk area. The next day, 71 flew a *Circus* and the last offensive sorties of the month were flown on the 27th when Hurricanes and bombers were escorted to Boulogne. This raid was led by the new CO, C.G. Peterson, who took over the squadron following the death of S/L Meares on the 15th when he collided with P/O R.O. Scarborough during a practice flight. Scarborough was also killed in the collision. Peterson had climbed to this position in a year after having joined the squadron as a pilot officer in November 1940. He was the first Eagle pilot to lead a RAF fighter squadron. He was replaced at the head of B Flight by P/O N. Anderson and, as P/O Daymond had taken over A Flight at the beginning of the month, the squadron was now entirely led by Americans from an operational point of view. December proved rather uneventful with about 150 sorties flown. A move to Martlesham Heath changed things up a bit, but got off to a good start when P/O E.M. Potter, from Minnesota, shared in a damaged Ju88 off Orford Ness with a pilot from No. 19 Squadron during a convoy patrol on 27th. The squadron had moved to its new station on the 14th and remained there for the next four and a half months.

In January, the squadron was involved in convoy patrols, with a couple of *Rhubarbs* and scrambles flown to break the routine. While not very intense for the American pilots, they flew close to 400 sorties despite the last week of January being washed out by bad weather. The squadron did make its mark during the month, however. During one of the few *Rhubarbs*, on the 9th, Pilot Officers E.M. Potter and R.S. Sprague (Washington State), the only participants on this op, each claimed one Fw190 destroyed three miles off Le Tréport. They were both newcomers who had only been with the squadron since the middle of autumn. Two days later, in the morning, F/O 'Sam' Mauriello and Californian P/O L.S. Nomis scrambled to 8000 feet to intercept a lone enemy aircraft. Several vectors were given by the Controller and the section became separated in cloud. After receiving further vectors, Nomis found himself well out to sea and, flying at 12,000 feet, turned for home. He saw a Ju88 breaking through a 10/10ths cloud layer at 11,000 feet and about 600 yards to his right. He immediately attacked it from the beam to the right quarter with a two second burst. Nomis saw pieces falling off the right wing of the Junkers. Then he directed his fire towards the cockpit of the Ju88 and saw some of his bullets striking home. Almost immediately the enemy aircraft dived into cloud cover and was not seen again. On returning to the base, Nomis claimed the aircraft as damaged. The bad weather at the end of January made the aerodrome unserviceable until 16 February. After three weeks of inactivity, 71 was ordered to scramble at 11.30 to intercept an enemy aircraft. Flying Officer C.L. Martin, from Pennsylvania, saw a Do217, but lost it almost immediately in cloud. Less than one hour later, another section took off on another scramble, but was recalled after ten minutes. A base patrol was followed by further scrambles, but nothing happened until the middle of the afternoon when Green Section, Pilot Officers Coen and H.L. Stewart (from North Carolina), saw a Do217 attempting to attack a convoy. The two American pilots attacked at once and fired all of their ammunition. The Dornier was hit and the Americans saw the aircraft entering cloud with black smoke pouring from it. Soon after they saw another Dornier that found cloud cover before they could make an attack. Green Section then returned to base where Coen filed a combat report for a damaged Do217. Uneventful convoy patrols were carried out the next day and, on the 24th, P/O J.J. Lynch from Ohio and P/O H.F. Marting from Indiana flew a Rhubarb over France where they strafed some ground targets, soldiers and a train, but no enemy aircraft were encountered. Lynch brought back a piece of telegraph pole in his wing proving that he flew very, very low! At the end of the month,

'Pete' Peterson was an American from Idaho. Eager to fight in Europe, he sailed to the UK during the summer of 1940, in the middle of the Battle of Britain, where he joined the RAF in August. The USAAC training he had already received helped him to speed up his training and he was soon posted to the newly-formed No. 71 (Eagle) Squadron in November. The squadron was the first fighter unit to group the pilots coming from the USA together. In May 1941 he became a flight commander and on 6 July he opened his score by claiming a probable Bf109. It was his only claim on the Hurricane as the squadron converted to the Spitfire soon after. In the following weeks his tally increased, opening the way to a DFC awarded in October, and in November he was called to lead the squadron. He held this position until 71 was transferred to the USAAF as the 334th FS in September 1942. Just before his transfer he was awarded the DSO and became the only 'Eagle' pilot to be honoured with this decoration. At the date of his transfer to the USAAF he had claimed six confirmed enemy aircraft destroyed, three more probables and six damaged. He continued the war by leading the 4th FG, the regrouping of the former 'Eagle' squadrons, and adding two more confirmed victories to his credit. He survived the war and continued his career in the USAF before retiring as a Major General in 1965.

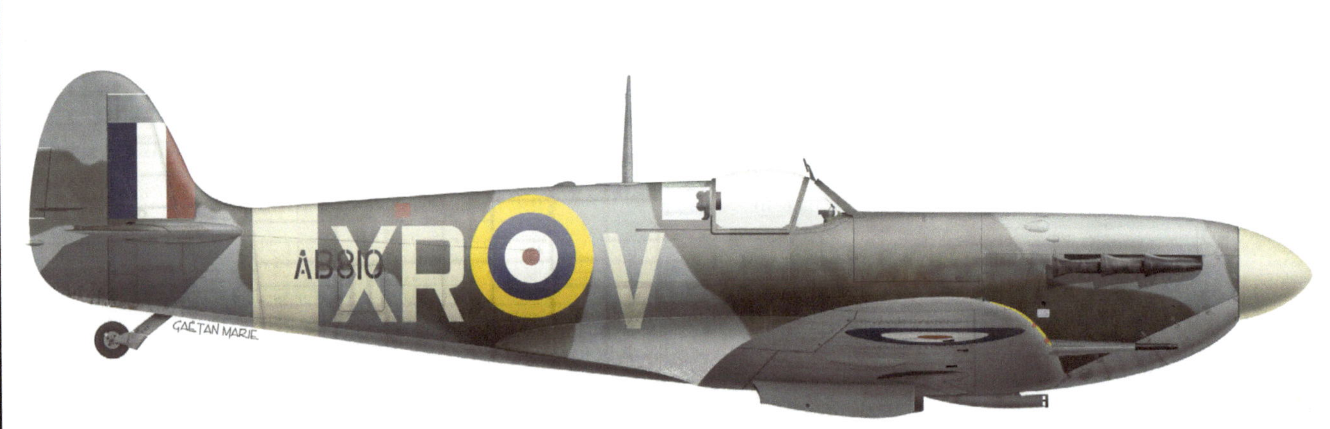

Supermarine Spitfire Mk VB AB810
No. 71 (Eagle) Squadron
Flight Lieutenant C.G. Peterson
North Weald (UK), September-October 1941

Frank Zavakos, from Idaho, was the son of Greek immigrants. He had enlisted in the USAAC in October 1940, but, after May 1941, he unexpectedly dropped out to apply to join the RAF through the Clayton Knight Committee. The fact that Greece had just collapsed and been occupied at that time is an indicator as to how he reached his decision while the US was still neutral in the European conflict. Having about 270 hours flying logged helped him speed up his training and he joined 71 Sqn in December 1941 and would serve with the unit until his death on 2 June 1942. *(www.greeks-in-foreign-cockpits.com)*

F/L Daymond, on long leave, was replaced at the head of A Flight by Sam Mauriello. Despite two weeks of inactivity, the squadron flew 230 sorties in February. In March, it completed close to 300 sorties, but the pilots had to wait until the 26th to break the monotony of the convoy patrols they were flying. That day, Black Section (Pilot Officers F.P. Dowling and Canadian-born American W.T. O'Regan) scrambled to patrol at 5000 feet. They soon spotted a lone enemy aircraft and Dowling fired two bursts, but observed nothing. The section was recalled immediately as there was doubt as to the identity of the aircraft. The month ended with a *Rhubarb* flown by F/L Anderson and P/O T.J. Andrews, but they returned to base with nothing to report.

In April, with spring and its favourable weather, activity increased steadily and, with more than 600 sorties flown, the squadron was more than adequately employed! In the first nine days, operational activity consisted of convoy patrols or scrambles and the pilots had to wait until the 10th to operate over the Continent when an uneventful *Rodeo* was flown. Two days later, a *Circus* went to Hazebrouck where the Luftwaffe was encountered and a quick dogfight took place. The Americans were not in a good position to make any claims and only one pilot was able to get a single burst in. The Germans, with the advantage, had more luck and shot down P/O B.F. Mays from Texas. The squadron flew a fighter sweep on the 14th followed by two *Circuses* on the 15th and a *Rodeo* on the 16th during which P/O O.H. Coen managed to damage a Fw190. The next morning, 71 returned to convoy patrols and, on the first one, P/O J.J. Lynch and P/O L.S. Nomis saw a lone Ju88. They both gave a chase but, while closing in, the German rear gunner hit Lynch's Spitfire and he was obliged to break off and return to base where he crashed and was injured. During that time, Nomis continued to engage and ran out of ammunition. His final burst must have been a good one as when he pulled away he saw the bomber diving into the sea. The same day, the squadron participated in a late morning *Circus* and a *Rodeo* in the middle of the afternoon, but each time the pilots returned with nothing to report. Defensive work was the routine over the following days until the 24th when a bomber escort (*Ramrod*) was flown. This was followed by two more the next day and the day after. During the last one, P/O R. McMinn (Oklahoma) ran out of fuel and was lucky to make a crash landing at Manston on return. He escaped injury, but that was to be the last flight for his Spitfire. On the 27th, the squadron escorted Hurribombers to Saint-Omer. The Luftwaffe tried to interfere over the target, but 71 did its job of protecting the Hurricanes. Squadron Leader Peterson managed to shoot down two Fw190s, and damaged a third, while P/O Coen, and M.G. McPharlin from Illinois, claimed the destruction of three others that they shared between them. Pilot Officer 'Art' Roscoe added a probable to the tally while Pilot Officers R.S. Sprague and E.M. Potter each claimed one Fw190 damaged. On the debit side, P/O J.V. Flynn from Illinois was posted missing, victim of the Fw190s, while P/O

J.A. Gray from California returned to base with such damage to his aircraft that it was declared beyond economical repair. On the 28th, the squadron escorted bombers in the middle of the morning and, in the afternoon, flew convoy patrols. The following day, only offensive ops were flown including a *Circus* that, upon the squadron's return to base, saw P/O Nomis make a bad landing. The Spitfire overturned in soft ground and was wrecked. The last two days of April were also busy, with one *Circus* and two scrambles on the 29th, and then two scrambles, one *Ramrod*, and a *Circus* to Abbeville, during which two more claims for damaged Fw190s were added by S/L Peterson and F/L Mauriello.

In May, activity decreased to a little more than 200 sorties, but the squadron reached the 5000 sortie mark since its formation in November 1940. In that time it had been one of the most active Fighter Command units. The squadron was now operating from Debden. It was a low scoring month with one probable over an unidentified aircraft during a bomber escort to Hazelbrouck on the 9th claimed by P/O Coen, and a Fw190 damaged on the 19th by the CO. Aside from the convoy patrols, 71 also flew ten bomber escorts, six fighter sweeps and a *Rhubarb*.

June began with two new flight commanders, G.A. Daymond returning to the head of his flight, while Oscar Coen took over B Flight. Three claims were made on the first day of the month, one confirmed and one damaged for Peterson, one confirmed for Daymond (initially claimed as damaged), and one each damaged for Pilot Officers R.S. Sprague and E.M. Potter. Those combats took place as part of the Debden Wing (with Nos. 350 and 111 Squadrons) which was despatched to escort eight Hurribombers. The squadron was flying middle cover at 23,000 feet, with 111 Squadron at 20,000 and the Belgians at 25,000 feet. The combat was not, however, one-sided as Californian P/O G. Teicheira failed to return. The next day, 71 was called to participate in an ASR mission, one flight relieving another in sequence. At 08.30, B Flight, led by F/L Coen, took off and, during the trip, the engine of the Spitfire flown by P/O Zavakos (Ohio) caused trouble. He was seen to crash into the sea thirty miles from Martlesham Heath. He did not survive the crash. The squadron participated in further ops over the Continent in June, but opportunities to fire at German aircraft were rare and no claim was made. The only occasion occurred on the 20th when P/O J.F. Helgason, from California, fired at a Fw190, but observed no results. July, however, was a bit special. The squadron was kept at readiness until the 8th. After that, operations were discontinued and the squadron declared non-operational prior to being posted overseas. This order was cancelled soon after. Flying activity resumed on the 15th, but only training flights were flown. Despite being at readiness during the following days, nothing happened on the operational side of things. However, luck was with Pilot Officers J.J. Lynch and J.F. Helgason on the 19th when the North Weald Wing came to Debden early in the afternoon to join the Debden Wing on a *Rhubarb*. As their unit had been released for the whole day for training duties, the two 71 Squadron pilots had, coincidentally, just taken off for a local flight. They took the opportunity to latch onto the Spitfires of No. 222 Squadron and headed to Dunkirk. Near Dunkirk, they headed towards Nieuport, the two Eagles flying in wide echelon. Lynch and Helgason then turned with the Wing to the right, through 180°, and flew back along the coast. On the turn, Lynch and Helgason were between the Wing and the coast. As they flew west along the coast, two Fw190s broke cloud in a dive, shallowing out so they approached head on. When within range Lynch fired a short burst at the Fw190 farthest from the coast. The German was already firing at someone, but the sudden appearance of Lynch made him stop. As the Fw190 passed, Lynch looked back and saw it half-rol-

Joe M. Kelly from California (left) and Edward T. Miluck from North Dakota (right). Like many Eagle pilots, the lack of opportunities forced them to volunteer to serve overseas. Kelly and Miluck flew in Africa in 1942 before being transferred to the USAAF in December 1942 and January 1943 respectively. Neither pilot was required for combat operations again.

'Chief' Nomis on the wing of his Spitfire. Note the Indian chief painted on the aircraft. He chose this personal artwork as his father was part Sioux Indian. Nomis did not transfer at the same time as his squadron mates and was posted to Malta in August 1942. He later served in North Africa with 92 Sqn. He finally transferred to the USAAF in March 1943, but was sent Stateside. He was medically discharged in July 1944 because of wounds received while in Tunisia. After the war he flew for the Chinese Air Force, from 1950 to 1951, and the Indonesian Air Force from 1952 to 1954.

ling onto its back. Before turning he looked ahead and saw four more Fw190s just below the cloud and approaching head-on. He pulled up, firing a burst into the group which split up as it passed overhead. At the same time, Helgason also opened fire at an oncoming Fw190. Lynch then had to pull up into cloud to avoid a section of Spitfires. Helgason by this time had called that his engine was causing trouble and when Lynch broke cloud again the sky was clear. Eventually both pilots managed to return to base and could file a claim for a destroyed Fw190 shared between them as a call from Wing Commander Scott-Malden reported that he and his pilots had seen it going into the sea.

The squadron was released for daily training later in the day until the 21ˢᵗ when a *Rhubarb* was flown by twelve aircraft over the Blankenberge-Dunkirk area. Further fighter sweeps were carried out until the end of the month and P/O Sprague was almost shot down by ground fire on the 24ᵗʰ. Fortunately, he managed to return to base uninjured, but the aircraft had been badly hit. Activity returned to normal in August with 230 sorties flown. On the first day of August, 71 was called to carry out Air Sea Rescue patrols with the sections relieving each other. These were to prove fruitful as enemy aircraft were encountered. Pilot Officer Gray, from California, fired at a Fw190 which disintegrated in mid-air while P/O Sprague gave chase to a Fw190 and fired a short burst. At that moment he was attacked from the rear and had to break away without having time to finish the job. Nevertheless, he was able to see that black smoke had started to come from the Fw190 and it was claimed as damaged. Later that day, Sprague (Red One) crashed on take off after the undercarriage collapsed. He survived unscathed and the Spitfire was found to be repairable. Pilot Officer H.D. Hively (Red Two) from West Virginia continued the sortie alone. The next few days were spent mainly in training, but, sadly, P/O J.F. Helgason was killed while practicing low level attacks on a gun position on the 6ᵗʰ. Until the 19ᵗʰ, the squadron was on the offensive only twice with a *Circus* and a *Roadstead*. Between the 14ᵗʰ and the 20ᵗʰ the unit operated from Gravesend, the base it would occupy for Operation *Jubilee*. The squadron participated in this combined operation with its first sortie taking off at 04.50 to cover the anchorage. Pilot Officer Strickland became separated from the others. He continued on alone and spotted a Fw190 having a sniff around. He attacked it and, before losing it in the gloom, knocked some pieces off it ten miles west of Dieppe before returning to land at Gravesend at 06.00. The rest of the formation was also involved in dogfights and Hawaiian P/O B. Morgan was separated from the others and encountered a Fw190 which made a firing pass at him. He managed to lose it and rejoined the squadron soon after. The CO then ordered him home as his aircraft had a glycol leak. He eventually made a wheels-up landing at Friston. A second sortie was flown soon after, the squadron being airborne at 10.45, Peterson leading again. During this sortie, he damaged a Ju88. The squadron was back on the ground at 12.25 and airborne again at 13.15. Peterson led again and opened fire on a Ju88. Duke-Woolley, at the head of the Debden Wing, saw it go into the sea to confirm Peterson's claim. However, the German rear gunner managed to fire a precise burst into Peterson's Spitfire. Smoke rapidly started to fill the cockpit and he was forced to bale out. Fortunately, he was rescued later in the day. Meanwhile, the other pilots were now involved in fierce combat with the Fw190s. Flight Lieutenant Coen and Pilot Officer M.G.H. McPharlin shared in the probable destruction of a Fw190 that was initially claimed as damaged. However McPharlin was hit in turn and also had to bale out. He was picked by a naval vessel. Finally, the squadron flew a fourth op between 17.15 and 18.55, but this proved uneventful. It participated in a *Circus* with the Wing the following day (*Circus* 206) and then another Wing-strength op the next day. Activity backed off after that until the 27th when the squadron flew a *Circus* to Saint-Omer. Enemy aircraft were encountered and W/C Duke-Woolley and 71 Squadron's new OC, S/L Daymond, each claimed a Fw190, while P/O A.J. Seaman (South Carolina) claimed a probable that was later downgraded to damaged. These were to be the last claims made by 71 Squadron. Sadly, they were balanced against the loss of Sergeant J.E. Evans from Ohio who was shot down and killed by the Fw190s. The squadron flew *Circus* 211 on the 28th, but no claims were made despite numerous combats. On the last day of August, two Spitfires took off at 17.10, P/O Stanley Anderson leading P/O W.D. Taylor from Massachusetts, for a *Rhubarb*. Taylor's aircraft was hit by ground fire while strafing a German flak ship off the Belgian coast and he abandoned his aircraft twenty miles off Blankenberge. He was later observed climbing into his dinghy. The next day, ASR work was carried out and a Defiant from an ASR squadron located him in the morning. However, the weather was closing in and it became impossible for the Walrus to try to pick him up. Another try was made in the afternoon, but Taylor could not be located. He was never seen again. He was to become the last of 71 Squadron's pilots to be killed in action. The next major action for the unit took place on the 5th when it participated with the Wing in a diversion raid for 36 Eighth Air Force B-17 Flying Fortresses, the bombers breaking away to Rouen while the Wing went to Le Tréport. A few enemy aircraft were seen, but did not attack. Two more diversion operations were carried out over the next two days and both were uneventful. The squadron was then placed on readiness for the next few days prior to its pending transfer to the USAAF on the 29th. It was on the 23rd that operational activity resumed with a fruitless scramble in the early hours flown by F/O W.J. Hollander, a Hawaiian, and P/O H.D. Hively. During the next days, the squadron flew some patrols and shipping reconnaissance sorties and avoided any losses before the transfer took place. The last sorties as 71 Squadron were flown on the 27th and involved a shipping reconnaissance led by F/L R.S. Sprague. Two days later, the squadron became the 334th Fighter Squadron of the USAAF.

September 1942, when many of the pilots serving with the squadron were transferring to the USAAF and thus wearing their new American uniforms. Left, Gordon H. Whitlow from Wyoming and, right, Robert L. Priser from Ohio. Both officially transferred on 15.09.42. Whitlow was killed in action nine months later (21.05.43) as a 334th FS member flying a P-47C-5.

Gregory A. Daymond
RAF No. 84657

'Gus' Daymond was one of the youngest Eagle pilots when he joined No. 71 (Eagle) Squadron in the autumn of 1940. From Montana, he joined the RAF via Canada during the summer. Sailing to the UK, he attended an OTU course and was posted to the newly formed 71 Squadron in November 1940. The unit started slowly; it was not until the spring of 1941 that it truly became operational on Hurricanes. For Daymond, things really changed when he made his first claim, a Bf109 destroyed near Lille on 2 July. Other claims soon followed on Hurricanes, then on Spitfires; his fifth victory was achieved on 4 September. In October, he was awarded the DFC. The next month, he became a flight commander and eventually took over the squadron at the end of August 1942, the same day he made his last claim with the RAF, an Fw190 destroyed over the northern French coast on 27 August, to bring his total to seven confirmed victories and one damaged. He transferred to the USAAF at the end of September 1942, adding a Bar to his DFC at the same time. Daymond served with the USAAF until the end of the war.

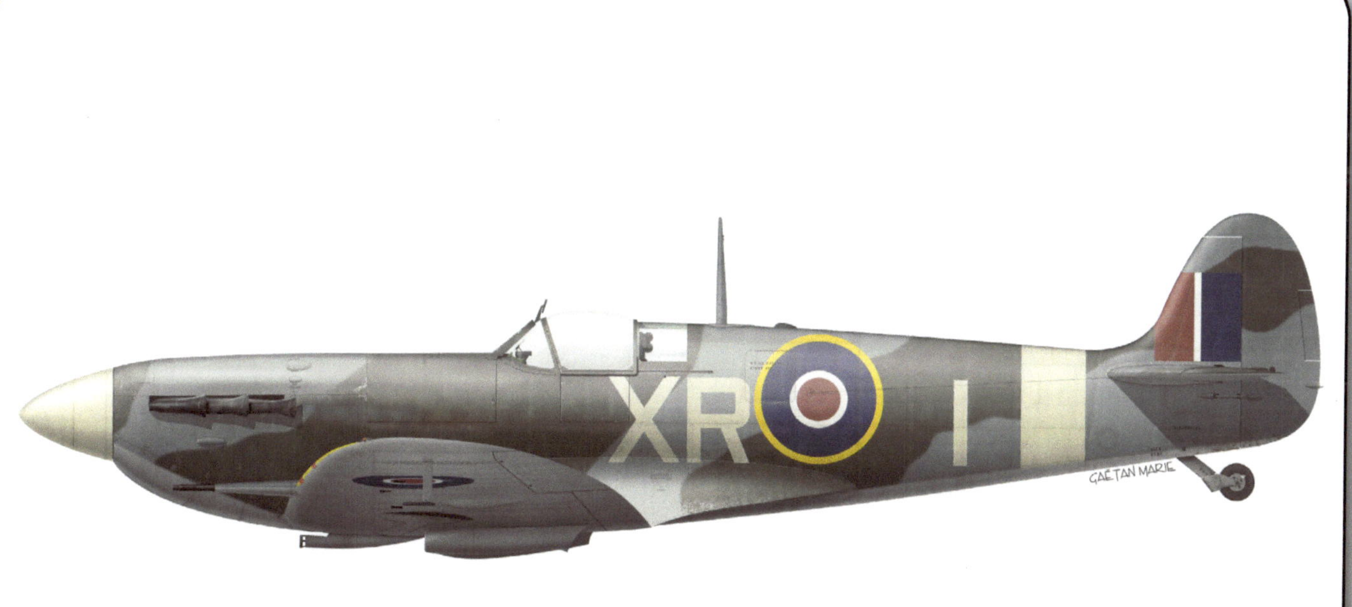

Supermarine Spitfire Mk VB EN915
No. 71 (Eagle) Squadron
Debden (UK), August-September 1942

Date	Pilot	SN	Origin	Type	Serial	Code	Nb	Cat.
	HURRICANE MK II							
15.05.41	P/O John K. **ALEXANDER**	RAF No. 86618	(US)/RAF	Bf109	**Z2756**		1.0	P
02.07.41	S/L Henry de C.A. **WOODHOUSE**	RAF No. 34189	RAF	Bf109	**Z3345**	XR-H	1.0	C
	P/O William R. **DUNN**	RAF No. 60510	(US)/RAF	Bf109	**Z3781**	XR-A	1.0	C
	P/O Robert L. **MANNIX**	RAF No. 64864	(US)/RAF	Bf109	**Z3335**	XR-F	1.0	P
	P/O Gregory A. **DAYMOND**	RAF No. 84657	(US)/RAF	Bf109	**Z3185**		1.0	C
06.07.41	P/O Gregory A. **DAYMOND**	RAF No. 84657	(US)/RAF	Bf109	**Z3829**		1.0	C
	F/L Chesley G. **PETERSON**	RAF No. 83706	(US)/RAF	Bf109	**Z3170**		1.0	P
	P/O William R. **DUNN**	RAF No. 60510	(US)/RAF	Bf109	**Z3267**		0.5	P
	Shared with P/O L. Jaugsch of No.306 (Polish) Sqn.							
19.07.41	P/O Victor R. **BONO**	RAF No. 85220	(US)/RAF	Bf109	**Z3266**		1.0	P
21.07.41	P/O William R. **DUNN**	RAF No. 60510	(US)/RAF	Bf109	**Z3781**	XR-A	1.0	C
02.08.41	P/O Gregory A. **DAYMOND**	RAF No. 84657	(US)/RAF	Do17	**Z3182**		1.0	C
09.08.41	P/O William R. **DUNN**	RAF No. 60510	(US)/RAF	Bf109	**Z3267**	XR-D	1.0	C
19.08.41	P/O Morris W. **FESSLER**	RAF No. 88385	(US)/RAF	Bf109	**Z3829**		1.0	P
	SPITFIRE MK II							
27.08.41	P/O William R. **DUNN**	RAF No. 60510	(US)/RAF	Bf109	**P7308**	XR-D	2.0	C
	SPITFIRE MK V							
04.09.41	P/O Thomas C. **WALLACE**	RAF No. 61933	(US)/RAF	Bf109	**AB783**		1.0	C
	P/O Gregory A. **DAYMOND**	RAF No. 84657	(US)/RAF	Bf109	**AB811**		1.0	C
	P/O Robert L. **MANNIX**	RAF No. 64864	(US)/RAF	Bf109	**AD123**		1.0	P
07.09.41	F/L Chesley G. **PETERSON**	RAF No. 83706	(US)/RAF	Bf109	**W3627**		1.0	C
18.09.41	F/L Chesley G. **PETERSON**	RAF No. 83706	(US)/RAF	Bf109	**W3627**		1.0	C
19.09.41	P/O Gregory A. **DAYMOND**	RAF No. 84657	(US)/RAF	Bf109	**AB812**		1.0	C
	P/O John **FLYNN**	RAF No. 61956	(US)/RAF	Bf109	**AB907**		1.0	C
21.09.41	P/O Caroll W. **MCCOLPIN**	RAF No. 61926	(US)/RAF	Bf109	**AB908**	XR-Y	1.0	C
	P/O Charles W. **TRIBKEN**	RAF No.64866	(US)/RAF	Bf109	**AD123**		1.0	P
27.09.41	F/L Chesley G. **PETERSON**	RAF No. 83706	(US)/RAF	Bf109	**AB810**	XR-V	1.0	P
	P/O Sam A. **MAURIELLO**	RAF No. 87010	(US)/RAF	Bf109	**AB783**		1.0	C
	P/O James J. **CROWLEY** *(J.G. DuFour)*	RAF No. 89765	(US)/RAF	Bf109	**AD123**		1.0	P
	P/O Ross O. **SCARBOROUGH**	RAF No. 65976	(US)/RAF	Bf109	**AB896**		1.0	C
02.10.41	S/L Stanley T. **MEARES**	RAF No. 37683	RAF	Bf109	**W3819**		1.0	C
	P/O Newton **ANDERSON**	RAF No. 87008	(US)/RAF	Bf109	**AB896**		0.5	C
	P/O Ross O. **SCARBOROUGH**	RAF No. 65976	(US)/RAF		**W3627**		0.5	C
	P/O Arthur F. **ROSCOE**	RAF No. 100530	(US)/RAF	Bf109	**W3708**		1.0	C
	P/O Caroll W. **MCCOLPIN**	RAF No. 61926	(US)/RAF	Bf109	**AB908**	XR-Y	2.0	C
16.10.41	P/O Caroll W. **MCCOLPIN**	RAF No. 61926	(US)/RAF	Hs126	**AB827**		1.0	C
25.10.41	P/O Ross O. **SCARBOROUGH**	RAF No. 65976	(US)/RAF	Bf109	**AA857**		1.0	C
27.10.41	P/O Caroll W. **MCCOLPIN**	RAF No .61926	(US)/RAF	Bf109	**AA857**		2.0	C
07.11.41	P/O Thomas C. **WALLACE**	RAF No. 61933	(US)/RAF	Bf109	**W3708**		1.0	C
09.01.42	P/O Robert S. **SPRAGUE**	RAF No. 103412	(US)/RAF	Fw190	**BL376**		1.0	C
	P/O Eugene M. **POTTER**	RAF No. 100529	(US)/RAF	Fw190	**BL292**		1.0	C
17.04.42	P/O John J. **LYNCH**	RAF No. 103470	(US)/RAF	Ju88	**W3740**		0.5	C
	P/O Leo S. **NOMIS**	RAF No. 107775	(US)/RAF		**BL287**	XR-C	0.5	C
27.04.42	S/L Chesley G. **PETERSON**	RAF No. 83706	(US)/RAF	Fw190	**BL449**	XR-P	2.0	C

Date	Pilot	RAF No.	Nationality	E/A	Serial	Code	Score	P/C
	F/O Oscar H. **Coen**	RAF No. 62244	(US)/RAF	Fw190	AD564		0.5	C
	P/O Michael G.H. **McPharlin**	RAF No. 89764	(US)/RAF		W3709		0.5	C
	F/O Oscar H. **Coen**	RAF No. 62244	(US)/RAF	Fw190	AD564		0.5	C
	P/O Michael G.H. **McPharlin**	RAF No. 89764	(US)/RAF		W3709		0.5	C
	F/O Oscar H. **Coen**	RAF No. 62244	(US)/RAF	Fw190	AD564		0.5	C
	P/O Michael G.H. **McPharlin**	RAF No. 89764	(US)/RAF		W3709		0.5	C
	P/O Arthur F. **Roscoe**	RAF No. 100530	(US)/RAF	Fw190	BM293	XR-W	1.0	P
09.05.42	P/O Arthur F. **Roscoe**	RAF No. 100530	(US)/RAF	E/A	AB941		1.0	P
01.06.42	S/L Chesley G. **Peterson**	RAF No. 83706	(US)/RAF	Fw190	BL449		1.0	C
	F/L Gregory A. **Daymond**	RAF No. 84657	(US)/RAF	Fw190	BL583		1.0	C
19.07.42	P/O John J. **Lynch**	RAF No. 103470	(US)/RAF	Fw190			0.5	C
	P/O Joseph F. **Helgason**	RAF No. 114001	(US)/RAF				0.5	C
01.08.42	P/O James A. **Gray**	RAF No. 108634	(US)/RAF	Fw190	AD288		1.0	C
19.08.42	F/L Oscar H. **Coen**	RAF No. 62244	(US)/RAF	Ju88	BM293	XR-W	0.5	P
	P/O Michael G.H. **McPharlin**	RAF No. 89764	(US)/RAF		W3767		0.5	P
27.08.42	S/L Gregory A. **Daymond**	RAF No. 84657	(US)/RAF	Ju88	BM510	XR-A	1.0	C

Total: **53.5**

Two other American pilots who held a flight commander position with 71 Sqn. Left, Bob Sprague and, right, Sam Mauriello. Sprague transferred in September 1942 and remained with the newly formed 4th FG with the rank of captain and flight leader. Sadly, he was killed in a mid-air collision on 26 November. Sam Mauriello transferred too, but left the 4th FG in December at the end of his tour. He eventually finished the war in the China-Burma-India Theatre. He left the Army after the war.

William Robert D**UNN**

RAF No. 60510

When war broke out, 'Wild Bill' Dunn, from Minneapolis, immediately went to Canada to join the RCAF. He was told the RCAF was not accepting American citizens so switched to the Canadian Army and eventually joined the Seaforth Highlanders and, in December 1939, sailed for England. At the end of the Battle of Britain, the British needed pilots so the RAF tried to recruit Army and Navy personnel who had flying experience, which he had before joined up. By May 1941, his training was complete, and he was posted to No. 71 (Eagle) Squadron. He made his first claim on 2 July by shooting down a Bf109 over France. During the summer of 1941, Dunn became one of the unit's most successful pilots until he was wounded in action on 27 August 1941, flying a Spitfire, the same day he achieved ace status. Recovered, he served with the RCAF in Canada until transferred to the USAAF in June 1943; later on, over France, he would make his final claims. Dunn survived the war and continued to serve in the USAAF/USAF.

Hawker Hurricane Mk.IIB Z3267
No. 71 (Eagle) Squadron
Pilot Officer W.R. Dunn
North Weald (UK), summer 1941

Supermarine Spitfire Mk.IIA P7308
No. 71 (Eagle) Squadron
Pilot Officer W.R. Dunn
North Weald (UK), August 1941

Caroll Warren McColpin
RAF No. 61926

An American from New York State, 'Red' McColpin decided, when war began in Europe, to join the RAF. Contacting the Clayton Knight Committee in charge of recruiting American pilots for the RAF, he was selected, thanks to his earlier flight experience, and completed his training in Canada before sailing to the UK where he was posted to the second Eagle squadron, No. 121, as a founding member, in May 1941 following a short stay at No. 607 Squadron. The new unit was flying Hurricanes at the time and at the end of the summer he was posted to No. 71 (Eagle) Squadron after this unit suffered heavy losses. Two weeks after his arrival he managed to make his first claim, a Bf109 destroyed, on 21 September. In the next five weeks he added more claims, including two double claims, to reach ace status. In January 1942 he was awarded the DFC. At the end of that month he was posted to No. 133 (Eagle) Squadron as a flight commander, thereby becoming one of the very few Eagle pilots to have served with all three Eagle squadrons. With 133 he would add four claims to bring his total with the RAF to eight confirmed and two damaged. His last claims with the RAF were made on 17 May. On 1 September he took command of the squadron just before it was transferred to the USAAF to become the 336th FS. He continued to lead the 336th until December 1942 when he returned to the US. 'Red' McClopin completed another tour in 1944 with the 407th FG where he added three confirmed victories over Fw190s in a single mission and damaged one more. He continued to serve the USAAF after the war, reaching the rank of Major General, and retired in April 1968.

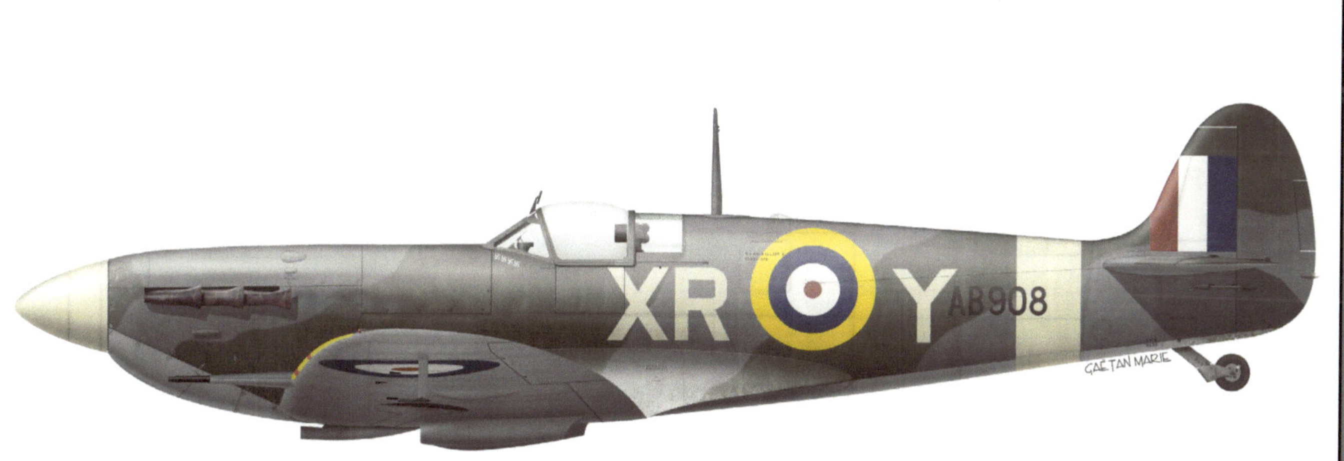

Supermarine Spitfire Mk VB AB908
No. 71 (Eagle) Squadron
Pilot Officer C.W. McColpin
Kirton-in-Lindsey, November 1941

Date	Pilot	S/N	Origin	Serial	Code	Fate
		HURRICANE MK I* & II				
09.02.41	P/O Edwin E. **ORBISON**	RAF No. 84659	(US)/RAF	**V6983***		†
15.02.41	P/O Vernon C. **KEOUGH**	RAF No. 81620	(US)/RAF	**V7606***		†
26.04.41	P/O James L. **McGENNIS**	RAF No. 84658	(US)/RAF	**Z2494**		†
15.05.41	P/O John **FLYNN**	RAF No. 61956	(US)/RAF	**Z2744**		-
17.05.41	P/O Stanley M. **KOLENDORSKI**	RAF No. 84875	(US)/RAF	**Z3186**		†
02.07.41	P/O William I. **HALL**	RAF No. 61921	(US)/RAF	**Z3094**		PoW
19.08.41	P/O Virgil W. **OLSON**	RAF No. 81619	(US)/RAF	**Z3494**		†
		SPITFIRE MK V				
07.09.41	P/O Hilliard S. **FENLOW**	RAF No. 61924	(US)/RAF	**AB900**		†
	P/O William H. **NICHOLS**	RAF No. 86619	(US)/RAF	**AB909**		PoW
	F/O Eugene Q. **TOBIN**	RAF No. 81622	(US)/RAF	**W3801**		†
	P/O Forrest P. **DOWLING**	RAF No. 100515	(US)/RAF	**AB815**		-
17.09.41	P/O Thomas P. **McGERTY**	RAF No. 61927	(US)/RAF	**W3509**		†
	P/O William D. **GEIGER**	RAF No. 64862	(US)/RAF	**W3763**	XR-L	PoW
13.10.41	P/O Gilmore C. **DANIEL**	CAN./ J.15016	(US)/RCAF	**AD112**		PoW
20.10.41	P/O Oscar H. **COEN**	RAF No. 62244	(US)/RAF	**AB827**		Eva.
27.10.41	P/O Morris W. **FESSLER**	RAF No. 88385	(US)/RAF	**AA855**	XR-C	PoW
12.04.42	P/O Ben F. **MAYS**	RAF No. 106509	(US)/RAF	**AB810**	XR-V	†
17.04.42	P/O John J. **LYNCH**	RAF No. 103470	(US)/RAF	**W3708**		-
25.04.42	P/O Richard **McMINN**	RAF No. 108641	(US)/RAF	**W3171**		-
27.04.42	P/O James A. **GRAY**	RAF No. 108634	(US)/RAF	**W3650**		-
	P/O John V. **FLYNN**	RAF No. 61956	(US)/RAF	**BM206**		†
29.04.42	P/O Leo S. **NOMIS**	RAF No. 107775	(US)/RAF	**BL287**	XR-C	-
01.06.42	P/O George **TEICHEIRA**	RAF No. 114074	(US)/RAF	**BM386**		†
02.06.42	P/O Frank G. **ZAVAKOS**	RAF No. 108645	(US)/RAF	**BM249**	XR-R	†
19.08.42	S/L Chesley G. **PETERSON**	RAF No. 83706	(US)/RAF	**BM361**	XR-C	-
	P/O Michael G.H. **McPHARLIN**	RAF No. 89764	(US)/RAF	**W3761**		-
27.08.42	Sgt Jack E. **EVANS**	CAN./ R.98138	(US)/RCAF	**AD196**	XR-Q	†
31.08.42	P/O William D. **TAYLOR**	RAF No. 115122	(US)/RAF	**BM305**		†

Total: 28

Left, Edwin Orbison from Oklahoma became the squadron's first operational casualty when he lost control of his aircraft during a patrol.
Right, Jack Evans from Ohio. Contrary to most American pilots of the Eagle Squadrons, he didn't passed by the Knight Committee to enlist in the RAF but enlisted in the RCAF instead like the majority of the Americans who wanted to fly and fight against the Nazis before the USA entered into war.

Above: 71's members awaiting a scramble. From left to right: Luke E. Allen, Charles E. Bateman, Hilliard S. Fenlaw and Newton Anderson. Fenlaw, from Texas, was killed while serving with the squadron on 7 September 1941 (see *SQUADRONS! 25*). Bateman became a flight commander with 133 Sqn but suffered sinus problems that resulted in him being sent to Canada as an instructor. In September 1944, he transferred to the USAAF.

Below: Thomas P. McGerty from California under the nose of a Hurricane shortly after his arrival at the squadron in April 1941. He was killed in action on 17 September 1941 while above Bateman and Fenlow are posing on the left and the right wings respectively.

Date	Pilot	S/N	Origin	Serial	Code	Fate
		HURRICANE MK I* & II				
01.01.41	P/O Vernon C. **KEOUGH**	RAF No. 81620	(US)/RAF	**P3459***		-
05.01.41	P/O Philip H. **LECKRONE**	RAF No. 84653	(US)/RAF	**V6636***		†
05.08.41	P/O William R. **DRIVER**	RAF No. 64869	(US)/RAF	**Z3266**		†
		SPITFIRE MK II				
08.08.41	P/O Kenneth S. **TAYLOR**	RAF No. 64869	(US)/RAF	**P8572**		†
		SPITFIRE MK V				
15.10.41	P/O Roger H. **ATKINSON**	RAF No. 102048	(US)/RAF	**AD123**		†
22.10.41	P/O Lawrence A. **CHATTERTON**	RAF No. 100987	(US)/RAF	**AA759**		†
15.11.41	S/L Stanley T. **MEARES**	RAF No. 37683	RAF	**W3963**		†
	P/O Ross O. **SCARBOROUGH**	RAF No. 65976	(US)/RAF	**W3627**		†
09.01.42	P/O William B. **INABINET**	RAF No. 108637	(US)/RAF	**AB783**		†
06.08.42	P/O Joseph F. **HELGASON**	RAF No. 114001	(US)/RAF	**W3709**		†

Total: 10

Phil 'Zeke' Leckrone from Illinois in a Spitfire of 616 Sqn during the Battle of Britain. He was one of the seven American fighter pilots to fly during that period. Having gained a lot of flying experience in the USA, he managed to get a shortened course when he enlisted in the RAF in Canada in July 1940. He was posted to 616 Sqn in early September 1940. He reported to 71 Sqn three weeks later and was sadly killed in a flying accident on 5 January 1941.

Victories - confirmed or probable claims: 26.0

First operational sortie:
02.08.41
Last operational sortie:
27.09.42

Number of sorties: ca. **3,150**

Total aircraft written-off: 29

Aircraft lost on operations: 22
Aircraft lost in accidents: 7

Squadron code letters:
AV

COMMANDING OFFICERS

S/L Robin P.R. Powell	RAF No. 33278	RAF	14.05.41	17.01.42
S/L Hugh C. Kennard	RAF No. 40396	RAF	17.01.42	31.07.42
S/L William D. Williams	RAF No. 78985	RAF	02.08.42	29.09.42

SQUADRON USAGE

The second American-manned squadron, 121, was formed at Kirton in Lindsey on 14 May 1941. As with 71, the CO and the flight commanders were initially British, S/L R.P.R. Powell, Flight Lieutenants H.C .Kennard (A Flight) and R.C. Wilkinson (B Flight and formerly of 71 Squadron) respectively. American pilots began to be posted in from various fighter squadrons, including 71. The first ten Hurricanes, all Mk.Is, were taken on charge on the 17th but only six were serviceable; it would not be until mid-June that 121 would get its full complement of pilots and aircraft. Training soon began, but, in June, things went wrong for several of the pilots. On the 15th, P/O R.F. Patterson suffered an engine failure and was obliged to abandon the Hurricane over Old Leake, 3 miles north-east of Boston. One week later, P/O L.L. Laughlin was killed when his aircraft dove into the ground north-west of Scampton. The cause of the accident was never discovered. In July, as more pilots continued to arrive, training continued, mainly on Hurricane Mk.IIs which were not only more powerful but also in better shape, being brand new. Two Mk.IIs were soon lost in a mid-air collision over Lincoln on the 27th. Pilot Officer W.V. Shenk and Sgt B. Smith both managed to bale out safely.

The squadron became operational at the end of July and on 2 August the first sorties were carried out; six scrambles were flown throughout the day. The Luftwaffe was very active over the area on the 8th and 121 was obliged to maintain a high level of activity with various convoy patrols and scrambles performed that day. While 15 miles north-east of Hull, P/O S.R. Edner and Sgt J.J. Mooney sighted a Ju88 and immediately gave chase. They closed in and both opened fire on the Junkers until their ammunition gave out. The Ju88 was seen to lose height during the combat from 2,500 feet to 300 feet. No one could ascertain its eventual fate, but it was credited as being probably destroyed and shared by the two pilots. One week after becoming operational, 121 had already opened its scoreboard. Another line was added ten days later when the CO claimed a Bf109 as probably destroyed 7 miles south of Gravelines during a fighter sweep with the wing over the Continent (involving twelve Spitfires from 121). It was the first sweep carried out by the unit. Three more sweeps were flown before the end of the month, but otherwise 121 remained busy with less challenging (and less dangerous) patrols for a grand total of about 175 sorties flown in August. The number of sorties was cut by half in September, but the squadron recorded a death on the 15th when P/O E.W. Mason was killed while practicing aerobatics. At the end of September, 121 moved to Digby for a few days but was soon back at Kirton in Lindsey. On 2 October, F/Sgt R.F. Tilley took off in the evening for a dusk patrol but got lost soon after; owing to an R/T failure, he decided to bale out near Burton. While he managed to get out of his Hurricane, his landing did not go well and he fractured a leg. The rest of the month was rather uneventful except that, halfway through, the first Spitfire Mk.IIs were taken on charge. Operational flying ceased and conversion began, 121 eventually becoming operational on the Spitfire at the end of the month after 350 operational sorties on Hurricanes. The last Hurricanes were flown out in November.

The Spitfire Mk II was, from the start, seen as an interim measure before Spitfire Mk.Vs were received and the squadron was sent south. The switch over took place from 19 October. The first local flights were carried out on the 19th and training continued until the end of the month without incident. On 1 November, the pilots heard they were to receive their first Mk.Vs before the end of the

Robin Peter Reginald POWELL
RAF No. 33278

Enlisting in the RAF before the war with a permanent commission, Powell was serving with No. 213 Squadron at the outbreak of war but was soon posted to No. 111 Squadron as a flight commander. He made his initial claim on 13 January 1940 in sharing the destruction of an He111 off Fifeness. During the next six months, he increased his score over France, Dunkirk, and England during the Battle of Britain, being awarded the DFC in May. At the end of July, he was posted out to in-struct and returned to operations in May 1941 to command No. 121 (Eagle) Squadron upon its formation. In January 1942, he was promoted to wing commander and became Wing Leader of the Hornchurch Wing; flying in that role, he made his last claim, an Fw190 destroyed on 2 June, but was wounded in action a few days later. In July, he added a Bar to his DFC. Once recovered, he served briefly in Tunisia before becoming Detling Wing Leader during the summer of 1944 and destroying two V-1s in July 1944. He remained in the role until October when he was in-volved in a car accident. Making it through recovery again, he eventually became OC No. 121 Wing in April 1945 as a Group Captain, a position he held until August. Powell continued to serve with the RAF after the war. His tally was nine confirmed victories (two shared), four unconfirmed or pro-bables, and four damaged, plus two V-1s.

Supermarine Spitfire Mk IIA P8186
No. 121 (Eagle) Squadron
Kirton-in-Lindsey (UK), November 1941

As was the case with many fighter squadrons formed during 1941, Eagle pilots worked up and commenced operations on Hawker Hurricanes. Above is Z3427/AV-R in which 'Sel' Edner shared a victory with John Mooney on 8 August 1941. But this Hurricane was in August 1941 regularly flown by P/O 'Red' McColpin.

month. Convoy patrols were flown that day with F/L Kennard leading the first pair. The squadron returned to its previous operational activities with the Hurricane while intense training continued. The first Spitfires were tested over the next few days. The Spitfire Mk.II began on ops, but this only lasted until 17 November when an uneventful scramble was flown by Mk.Vs. The Spitfire II lasted about a month with 121, but still managed to complete 57 sorties.

The first Spitfire Mk.Vs, AA903 and AA922, were flight tested on 6 November. More were taken on charge over the following days and subsequently tested. The first operational flights, four aircraft led by Wilkinson on a convoy patrol, were flown on the 16th. Another convoy patrol took off at noon and both were uneventful. The rest of the month consisted of convoy patrols and useless scrambles, but

An American pilot is preparing to jump into Spitfire P8136/AV-P for a practice flight. By November 1941, the Spitfire was about to be phased out from the front line squadrons.

it is worth noting that the first Mk.V Rhubarb flown by the squadron was a sweep over Holland on the 25th carried out by Virginian P/O R.F. Patterson and New Yorker Sgt J.J. Mooney. Both pilots returned safety, but Mooney's aircraft was slightly damaged.

December 1941 was far from a busy month with just 65 sorties carried out. Bad weather was partially responsible for this result. On the 7th, Pilot Officers Patterson and V.E. Watkins, the latter from California, went on a Rhubarb to the Belgian coast. The target was Knocke, but the two pilots hit the coast twenty miles west at a place called Blankenberge. They became separated for a moment and Watkins ended up returning home alone. Patterson never returned and was posted missing. It was later confirmed that he had been killed. The bad luck hung around the squadron as another pilot, Californian P/O K. LeR. Holder, was posted missing from a convoy patrol five days later. Although his body was later recovered, the cause of the crash was never determined.

The new year did not start well for the pilots of 121 when another of their number, P/O J.D. Gilliland from Illinois, was lost in a flying accident on the 8th when operating from Southend. The squadron was now based at Southend after a short stay at North Weald at the end of the 1941. He had taken off at 09.00 with eleven others, F/L Kennard leading, to proceed to Martlesham Heath for a convoy patrol. Sometime after take off, the weather was bad enough to force the formation to return home. Gilliland got lost and crashed in a street in Ipswich. He is believed to have mistaken the fog for cloud. Kennard took over the squadron on the 17th, relinquishing command of his flight to P/O V.E. Watkins. January was otherwise a fairly uneventful month with the squadron being occupied with convoy patrols and only six sorties, of 135 flown that month, being attributed to a single sweep on the 6th. The beginning of February continued in the same vein, but, on the 12th, the squadron participated in the failed attempt to sink two German battlecruisers, *Scharnhorst* and *Gneisenau*, and the heavy cruiser *Prinz Eugen*, as they audaciously ran the gauntlet of the narrow English Channel on their way to German ports during the infamous 'Channel Dash'. The squadron provided air cover for attacking aircraft, but all Spitfires returned to base without having engaged in combat. In the second part of February, 121 continued to carry out convoy patrols, but was engaged more frequently flying *Rhubarbs*, although the Luftwaffe was not seen. With the weather improving, especially after the first week of March, the squadron was airborne more often and 200 sorties were flown that month. On 12 March, the unit took part in a major sweep with the Wing. Heavy flak was experienced between Cassel and Poperinge and probably hit the Spitfire flown by P/O W.L.C. Jones (RCAF), an American from Maryland. He was last seen under control with glycol pouring from his aircraft. He was later reported as a PoW. The next day, the squadron was asked to escort minesweepers. While the patrol itself was uneventful, P/O R.W. Evans stalled and crashed on landing. The aircraft was a write-off and Evans suffered a fractured arm and broken jaw which kept him away from the squadron until mid-June. The same day, major changes occurred in the flight commanders' positions with P/O T.W. Allen, from South Carolina, and P/O C.L. Martin, from Pennsylvania, each receiving their flight lieutenant stripes and assuming the lead of A and B Flights respectively. Until the 23rd, the squadron was involved in uneventful convoy patrols. On the afternoon of the 23rd, a Wing sweep

Pilots of 121 Sqn marching for the camera with the 'Stars and Stripes' flag in the background. This photo was taken for propaganda purposes at the end of November just a few days before the USA entered war.

The pilots who can be identified are, from left to right: M.L. Stepp from California (killed 30.09.43 with the USAAF), L.A. Skinner from Missouri (PoW 28.04.42), D.W. McLeod from Massachusetts, behind, K.L. Holder from California (killed 12.12.41), H.C. Kennard, A Flight OC - British, F.A. Gamble from Tennessee (killed 03.05.42), S/L R.P.P. Powell, OC - British, V.A. Parker from Texas, R.E. McHan from Nebraska (who would not transfer to the USAAF), J.J. Lynch from Ohio, C.L. Martin from Pennsylvania, W.L.C. Jones from Maryland (PoW 08.03.42), R.F. Patterson from Virginia (killed 07.12.41) and W.J. Daley from Texas with head down (killed 10.09.44 with the USAAF).

No.121 Squadron soldiered on with Spitfire Mk.Vs for the last ten months of its brief existence. This is a very well known photo of BM590/AV-R, 'Olga', in flight. It was regularly flown by Gilbert O. Halsey, from Oklahoma, who joined the squadron in February 1942. At age 32, Halsey was the oldest Eagle pilot when he transferred to the USAAF in September 1942. He remained with the 335th FS until the end of his tour.

took place, but this time the Luftwaffe was keen to engage the RAF fighters. The other units involved were Nos. 22 and 403 Squadrons. It did not work out well for the attackers with a Fw190, claimed destroyed by P/O Mooney (RCAF), shot down a mile out to sea from Calais. This was the squadron's first confirmed kill since conversion to the Spitfire V. Mooney had also fired earlier at three other Fw190s without result. Pilot Officer W.J. Daley from Texas also fired at three enemy aircraft, but no results were obtained either. Flight Lieutenant Allen had a similar experience with a single Fw190. The next day, the same squadrons (121, 222, 403) were airborne in the early afternoon to accompany eight Bostons to their target at Comines. The Hornchurch, Northholt and Kenley Wings were also part of the game. The Eagles were ordered to protect the Hornchurch Wing and were flying between 15,000 and 16,000 feet when the Germans appeared. In the ensuing engagement, P/O R.F. Tilley (RCAF) from Florida got into a good position to fire at a Fw190. It was seen belching thick black smoke before diving into a cloud upside down. Tilley claimed it as a probable. Later on, while coming home, Tilley also fired at two other Fw190s, between the target and the French coast, without result. Pilot Officer Daley also used his guns on a Fw190, but was unable to register any hits. In this engagement, 121 did not sustain any direct loss to the Luftwaffe, but P/O L.A. Skinner, from Missouri, made a crash-landing at Deal after running out of fuel. The aircraft did not survive the crash, but Skinner was safe. Before the end of the month, the squadron took part in other Wing sweeps on the 25th, without incident, and on the 27th, but this ended prematurely after a misunderstanding with Control.

On 1 April, the squadron accompanied Nos. 22 and 403 Squadrons to escort twelve Bostons to bomb the docks at Boulogne. The squadron served as high cover, flying at 22,000 feet, but the Luftwaffe did not show up. The unit participated in further sweeps on the 2nd, 3rd, 4th, 8th and 10th, but those proved rather uneventful. Another sweep was flown on the 12th with the Debden and Hornchurch Wings also taking part. The task was, once again, an escort for twelve Bostons, but, contrary to the previous raids, at least as far as 121 Squadron was concerned, the enemy was engaged. The North Weald Wing was acting as close escort to the Bostons and 121 was flying at 10,000 feet when Fw190s intercepted the formation around Hazebrouck. Fierce combat ensued and in about ten minutes the Eagles had made six claims. Flight Lieutenant T.W. Allen, from South Carolina, claimed one probable and one damaged, while P/O L.A. Skinner from Missouri damaged two. The CO and Californian P/O J.B. Mahon claimed one damaged Fw190 each. These successes were claimed for no loss even though the aircraft of P/O Edner (Minnesota) returned with some flak damage. One of Skinner's claims was confirmed as destroyed two days later. Another sweep was carried out the next day, but the Germans were not sighted. Yet another was flown on the 14th and P/O Mooney was able to fire two bursts at a Bf109, but did not have the chance to see how effective he had been. On the 15th, the squadron was able to file some claims. After one diversionary sweep in the morning, 121 took part in another Wing sweep to escort Hurricane fighter-bombers. Combat occurred around Calais and Saint-Omer and two Fw190s were claimed destroyed, one by P/O S.R. Edner and one by P/O Skinner. Edner dived from 20,000 feet to 9,000 feet to attack his future victim, closing in to 400 yards before firing. He missed with his first three second burst so continued to follow the 190 to 7,000 feet where he fired for another three seconds and caused the Fw190 to burst into flames before it crashed into the ground. Skinner flew a similar attack and saw his Fw190 crash into the sea after a three second burst from 75 yards astern. Flight Lieutenant Allen got himself in to a good position to fire at another Fw190, but he did not see the results and only made a claim for a damaged Fw190 after his gun camera film was examined. The next day, the squadron was airborne again for one another sweep, but this time things went wrong as P/O R.V. Brossmer, from New York State, crashed on take off. His Spitfire turned over, but he was dragged out with nothing worse than cuts and bruises. The aircraft was repaired. Soon after, S/L Kennard had to return home when his canopy came off. He was followed by F/L Martin and

Hugh Charles KENNARD
RAF No. 40396

Hugh Kennard joined the RAF on a short service commission in October 1937. With his training completed, he joined No. 66 Squadron in August 1938. In October 1939, he was posted to No. 610 (County of Chester) Squadron, but was back with 66 in March 1940. On 12 May he opened his score by sharing in the destruction of a He111 over Holland. He participated in the Battle of Britain, but didn't have much success. At the end of August, he was posted to No. 306 (Polish) Squadron as a flight commander. In May 1941, he was sent to perform the same role with No. 121 (Eagle) Squadron, taking command of the unit in January 1942. In June he was awarded the DFC and made his last claim on 31 July, a Bf109 destroyed, to bring his score to four confirmed victories (three shared), one shared probable and one damaged. However, that same day he was wounded in combat and forced to relinquish command. From September 1942 onwards he held various HQ positions, but eventually returned to an operational role in May 1945 by taking command of No. 74 (Trinidad) Squadron as it was about to convert to the Meteor F.III. Remaining in this position until September, he continued to serve in the RAF until June 1946.

Supermarine Spitfire Mk VB BM581
No. 121 (Eagle) Squadron
Southend (UK), July 1942

Two pilots conversing after returning from an op: John Mooney from New York (left) and Don McLeod from Massachusetts. Mooney, a key pilot, was earmarked for greater responsibility and would likely have become CO if he had not been killed in action as a flight commander on 16 June 1942. McLeod, like Reade Tilley, left the squadron in March 1942 for Malta where he was severely wounded in combat. He returned to the UK at the end of July 1942 and transferred to the USAAF in September, but did not serve with the 4th FG.

P/O J.I. Brown (Illinois) who both returned early with engine trouble. On the 17th, the squadron was tasked with two ops. The first was an uneventful diversionary Wing sweep just before midday. They returned to the same area in the middle of the afternoon, flying as top cover at 27,000 feet. This time the Luftwaffe rose to fight. A melee soon developed and when the Germans extricated themselves, they had had the advantage as none of the participating Eagle pilots were able to make claims, but one pilot, F/Sgt F.C. Austin (RCAF) from California, was missing. After this intensive first fortnight, the pressure eased for the next few days and little flying was performed (none over the Continent). Bad weather was to blame and the pilots took the opportunity to rest. Ops resumed on the 24th. The Wing combined its strength with the Debden Wing and took off in the direction of France to escort twelve Bostons to attack the harbour and oil installations at Flushing in Belgium. After successfully escorting the bombers, Pilot Officers Daley and Skinner spotted what they thought to be a Ju52 transport aircraft. They peeled off, attacked it several times, and it began to trail white smoke and shed pieces. From above, the wing leader, W/C Scott-Malden, and P/O Allen watched as the enemy aircraft caught fire and went into the sea. Later on, when they compared notes and checked the photos of their cine-gun film, Daley and Skinner discovered they had shot down a venerable Junkers W-34. It was, however, credited as a Ju52. Another sweep was undertaken the next day and the Luftwaffe tried to intercept the raid. Only P/O Mooney was able to fire at a Fw190, but, as he did not see any result, no claim was made. However, P/O B.C. Downs from Texas encountered engine trouble and was forced to bale out over the sea four miles off Ramsgate. He was not picked up, but was able to paddle his dinghy safely to shore and was soon back with the squadron. Another dogfight occurred on the 28th during which F/O S.R. Edner made a claim against a Fw190. It was initially claimed as a probable, but was later downgraded to damaged. The Germans once again achieved a clear advantage over the Americans and P/O C.G. Bodding, from Kansas, was shot down and seen to bale out. Sadly, he was too low and was killed. It was not the only loss as P/O Skinner also had to bale out. He ended up in captivity. Another sweep was carried out on the 29th and was followed by three more on the 30th, one in the morning and two in the afternoon, but nothing came of those raids. In all, 426 sorties were flown in April and the squadron also celebrated flying 1000 sorties since its formation.

May was also intense even though the number of sorties decreased, 386 in May against April's 426. The squadron flew over French or Belgian territory almost every day of the month. The Luftwaffe was not seen each time and, when combat did occur, claims were not always forthcoming. On 4 May, near Le Havre, S/L Kennard shot at two Bf109s without result, as did F/L Allen against a Bf109. Pilot Officer Daley fired at another Bf109 and observed no result even though Allen and P/O Mahon saw the German spinning down pouring white smoke. The combat was fierce, however, but the Germans got the advantage over the Spitfires and two pilots were posted missing – Pilot Officers R.W. Freiberg from Minnesota and R.V. Brossmer from New York City. Flight Lieutenant Martin saw Freiberg's aircraft diving towards the sea about fifteen miles off Le Havre. He tried to call him over the radio, but got no answer. As for Brossmer, he was last seen by P/O Mooney leaving the French coast.

Until the 11th, the squadron was sent over the Continent every day, but no combats eventuated. The squadron was released from 13.00 on the 11th and, during the next few days, bad weather prevented further activity. The Eagles were airborne again on the 14th then released the next day because of the weather. Operations resumed on the 16th, but the day's Rhubarb was uneventful. The following day the squadron took off twice for sweeps to Boulogne with Nos. 222 and 331 Squadrons. For the first sweep, the Wing returned without incident, but, on the second one, while near Saint-Omer, P/O Edner saw a Fw190 and attacked from 190 yards with a one second burst. The Fw190 exploded. Almost immediately after, it was the turn of P/O Daley to spot and engage a Fw190. The attack was made from behind and above and P/O Daley fired a three second burst. The enemy fighter caught fire and was not seen again. Both claims were accepted as destroyed, while Pilot Officers Mooney and Mahon each claimed a Fw190 as damaged. On 20 May six aircraft were sent on a shipping reconnaissance with the aim of flying around Brankenburg. Finding nothing, they decided to fly towards Walcheren and soon after saw a German patrol vessel which opened fire at them. The six Spitfires dove from 6,000 feet to make several firing passes. The patrol boat was left severely damaged and disappeared before escorting Bf109s, which were flying too far away, could come to the rescue. Operations continued over the following days and another boat was attacked on the 26th. The next day, two minesweepers escorted by a destroyer became the target of the Eagles. They were attacked and damaged, but Bf109s made an appearance and went after P/O Daley and Sgt Vance. Daley attacked one of them and soon one Bf109 was seen to crash into the sea. Vance claimed another as damaged. Vance was not the only one to claim a Bf109 damaged as P/O Mahon did the same. The squadron flew operationally on the 28th and the 30th, but nothing of interest was reported. On the 31st, the North Weald Wing proceeded on a shipping reconnaissance off the coast of Flushing and two minesweepers were eventually attacked and damaged. In doing so, F/L Allen, who had made a steep dive attack, struck the water and ricocheted up to about 1000 feet. He announced over the R/T that his aircraft was coming apart and that he proposed to ditch at 100 mph. He did so at a rather steep angle and was not seen to emerge from the Spitfire, which sank immediately. It is thought that he may have been hit in the engine during the second attack as P/O 'Barry' Mahon stated that he saw glycol streaming from Allen's aircraft.

On 1 June, 121 took part in a Rodeo in the morning and a *Circus* in the afternoon. Operations continued over the next few days with 111 sorties carried out up to the 5th. No operations were flown during the next two days due to bad weather, but the squadron returned over the French coast on the 8th for a *Rodeo*. Near Saint-Omer, the unit engaged some Fw190s and F/L Mooney, the new B Flight CO, was the first to make a claim when he sent a Fw190 crashing to the ground. Immediately after this one, he attacked another Fw190 and shot it down in flames in a couple of seconds. At the same time, P/O Mahon sealed the fate of two other Fw190s, both being claimed as destroyed. These victories were the first double claims made by squadron pilots since the unit's formation. Also pleasing was that all Spitfires returned to base. On 14 June, the squadron flew a shipping reconnaissance and was just outside Ostend when they saw an armed trawler sailing four miles from the coast off Walcheren. Squadron Leader Kennard made two attacks at deck height as the vessel opened fire with machine guns mounted on the stern. Kennard then ordered the squadron to join in. The squadron made two more passes and eventually silenced the guns. During the second attack, a violent explosion was seen on the stern and thick black smoke issued from the vessel. It was seen to list heavily to starboard, decrease its speed and make for shore. After a convoy patrol on the morning of the 16th, F/L Mooney and P/O 'Sed' Edner headed out on a Rhubarb. They took off at 12.20 and travelled towards Ostend where a freight train was observed. They attacked it from astern, F/O Edner firing a four second burst. This resulted in the train being brought to a standstill and it appeared as though the driver had been killed. Immediately after this attack, F/L Mooney disappeared so Edner called him on his R/T, but it had gone u/s. He then circled the train twice, to see if there was any sign of F/L Mooney, but to no avail.

Flying Officer J.M. Osbourne from Virginia plays a tune on his banjulele as entertainment for his Eagle Squadron colleagues on the terrace of the old English house in which they are billeted. Left to right, the 'audience' is: Pilot Officer J.L. Kearney from Illinois (smoking a pipe), Pilot Officer J.T. Slater from New Jersey and Pilot Officer C.V. Padget from Maryland (seated on the window sill). All transferred to the USAAF and survived the war but John Slater who became the last 121's casualty of the war on 21 September 1942 but also one of the first 4th FG's casualty as he had transferred to the USAAF previously on 16 September.

An intelligence officer collects information from an Eagle Squadron Spitfire crew after a flight. Left to right, they are: Flying Officer E.D. Beatie from Georgia, Flight Lieutenant Seldon R. Edner, the intelligence officer, Squadron Leader W. R. Williams the CO, Pilot Officer D.A. Young from Kansas and Pilot Officer F.R. Boyles whose American background remains obscure except that he was born in Burma. He served with 133 for a very short time before joining 121 in June 1942. He transferred to the USAAF and was later killed in action on 8 April 1944. Behind Spitfire V EN918/AV-X usually flown by F/L Edner at the time.

Mooney was replaced at the head of B Flight by W.J. Daley. The squadron lost a second Spitfire in June, but by accident, when, on the 23rd, Virginian P/O J.M. Osborne hit the Blackwater River off Osea Island, Essex, while involved in low flying practice with five other aircraft. He survived and was picked up by fishing boats soon after. More operations were flown over the Continent until the end of the month, but nothing of note was reported. June ended quite smoothly with some uneventful convoy patrols. July, however, would be the busiest month for the squadron with 528 sorties carried out. Nevertheless, the first week was quiet and no major operations were flown. On the 8th, P/O G.O. Halsey (Oklahoma) and Sgt A.C. Stanhope (of French parentage) were scrambled at 07.10 and vectored to intercept a lone Ju88. They spotted it off Dunkirk and gave chase. It was not until the Junkers was over Cap Gris Nez that both pilots were able to attack. Halsey fired a four second burst from 400 yards line astern, but observed no results. Stanhope then fired from the same distance. At first it seemed impossible to catch the Junkers, but Stanhope gave it another burst from astern which caused it to weave. This gave him the opportunity to close in. Stanhope saw the rear gunner firing at him so fired another short burst from 300 yards to silence him. Closing in, he fired again from 80-90 yards and observed orange flashes coming from the port engine and thick smoke trailing from it. The Junkers then went into a cloud and Stanhope waited for it to emerge. He fired a final burst when it did and expended his ammunition. The two American pilots returned to base where they claimed the Ju88 as damaged.

Offensive operations were resumed from the 12th with a Rodeo followed by Rhubarbs on the 14th and 15th. The *Rhubarb* on the 15th was followed by a *Roadstead*. No enemy aircraft were encountered, but this was not the case for the *Rodeo* of the 19th as F/L S.R. Edner claimed a Fw190 as damaged. Only one other claim for a damaged aircraft was filed on the 30th (F/L W. Daley) despite numerous ops flown over the previous ten days. During that period, when eighty sorties were flown, the squadron did not suffer any losses, but one Spitfire was damaged by flak on the 22nd and its pilot, F/Sgt J.M. Sanders (RCAF) from Tennessee, was slightly injured in his right hand. On 31 July, twelve pilots took off at 14.10 for a *Circus*. The squadron was led by the CO. Landfall was made at Berck-sur-Mer and rendezvous with the North Weald and Tangmere Wings was made at Pevensey Bay. They had to escort six Bostons to Abbeville. The Luftwaffe decided to intervene and rose to intercept. The Eagles did not wait to be attacked and chased after several Fw190s encountered. The harvest of victories that followed was to be the best ever claimed by the unit to date. The CO claimed one Fw190 destroyed, while F/L Edner and Mahon each scored two destroyed. Two pilots opened their score that day. Sergeant W.P. Kelly from New York State claimed one aircraft destroyed and F.R. Boyles claimed a probable Fw190. These victories were obtained at a cost, however, as P/O N.D. Young, from Oregon, who had been with the squadron for only two weeks, was lost. The CO was also injured and had to crash land at Lynpne where he was taken to the hospital at Maidstone. While he recovered from his injuries, it put an end to his command and he did not lead another operational unit before the end of the war. He was replaced by British S/L W.D. Williams, posted from 122 Squadron, from August 2 onwards. In August, the squadron was airborne operationally for 25 days out of 31 and flew just over 300 operational sorties. Without a doubt the main event of the month was the unit's participation in Operation *Jubilee* on the 19th. Up to that date, the squadron had little to report upon return from their ops. On the famous day over Dieppe, the first operation was carried out in the morning, taking off at 08.40, in company with No. 19 Squadron. They patrolled over Dieppe at 5,000 feet and, less than 45 minutes after taking off, 121 was involved in various dogfights with Fw190s. The squadrons were split up and the pilots returned to base one by one or in pairs. It didn't take long to observe that three pilots were missing – P/O J.L. Taylor from Indiana, and Californians P/O J.B. Mahon and P/O G.B. Fetrow. Soon after, good news came from Fetrow who had been obliged to bale out over England, his aircraft on fire following hits from German fighters. Later on, it was discovered that Mahon had been shot down and become a PoW after he had shot down his fifth enemy aircraft (that he could not file as a claim). Sadly, for Taylor, the news was not good as he was presumed dead following a possible collision with a Fw190. On the other hand, one confirmed victory and two probables, along with a damaged claim by P/O F.D. Smith, a Texan, almost balanced the ledger. Despite its losses, the squadron was airborne again at 11.50, again with 19 Squadron, but the weather deteriorated quickly forcing the pilots to fly below 2,500 feet and, therefore, in range of light flak. One Spitfire, F/L Daley's, was hit. While 19 Squadron engaged the enemy, 121 was not as lucky and came close to losing a fourth Spitfire when Daley's engine stopped a few seconds after being hit. He was preparing to bale out when the engine restarted. A third op was carried out in the late afternoon, but proved uneventful except that P/O J.M. Osborne crashed back at base when the undercarriage collapsed on landing. Following Dieppe, 121 continued to fly operational sorties, almost 95 of them before the end of the month, including 29 on the 24th. However, no further combats or losses were reported.

In September, operational activity decreased pending the future transfer to the USAAF at the end of the month. The number of sorties was almost cut by half. On 1 September, two sections received orders to intercept a lone Ju88. The German reconnaissance bomber was sighted once, but it disappeared into cloud and was not seen again. Early in the month, F/L Edner received notification that he had been awarded the DFC, the last of four pilots, following Kennard, Daley and Mahon, to be so awarded while flying with 121 Squadron. The first sweep of September was performed on the 5th towards Abbeville, but was uneventful. The squadron flew a diversionary sweep the next day and, on the 7th, engaged the Luftwaffe, but no claim was made by the two pilots who nevertheless were able to get in to good positions to open fire (Pilot Officers Fentrow and Stanhope). That was to be the last engagement against the Luftwaffe for the squadron as it flew convoy patrols or shipping recces from then on. During one such sortie on the 21st, 121 lost its last aircraft and pilot when New Jersey native P/O Slater was hit in the glycol tank by fire from a flak ship. He was flying with P/O W.P. Kelly (RCAF) and they had attacked the ship and left it burning. Kelly saw Slater, who was posted missing, crash into the sea. Two days later, the squadron moved to Debden to become the 335th Fighter Squadron of the 4th Fighter Group, USAAF.

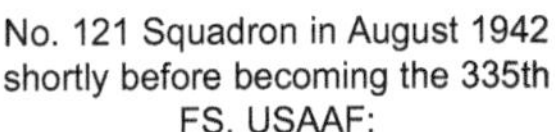

No. 121 Squadron in August 1942 shortly before becoming the 335th FS, USAAF:
Pilot Officer J.M. Osborne from Virginia shares his experience of a dogfight, following a fighter sweep, with other members of the Eagle Squadron. Left to right are: F.D. Smith from Texas, J.M. Sanders from Tennessee, D.A. Young from Kansas, P/O Osborne, S/L W.D. Williams (RAF), C.V. Padget from Maryland, G.B. Fetrow from California, F.R. Vance (RCAF) from Washington D.C. who did not transfer (killed 13.07.43), G.O. Halsey from Oklahoma, P/O F.R. Boyles born in Burma from American parentage (with the cigarette and a shoulder badge 'U.S.A.' instead of the usual Eagle badge – killed 28.07.43 with the USAAF), S.R. Edner from Minnesota (just visible), W.J. Daley from Texas, J.R. Happel from New Jersey, and J.B. Mahon from California (PoW 19.08.42).

William Dudley WILLIAMS

RAF No. 78985

Joining the RAFVR in about April 1938 as an 'airman under training', Williams was called to full-time service at the outbreak of war. He joined No. 152 Squadron in May 1940 with a commission. He saw action during the Battle of Britain, making eight claims between 13 August and 30 September. In January 1941, Williams received the DFC and, on 14 March, damaged a Ju88 in combat for his final claim, bringing his tally to six confirmed victories (one shared) and three damaged. In August, he became a flight commander. Finally, in October 1941, he was rested and served as a flight instructor.

Williams started a second tour of operations in May 1942, joining No. 122 (Bombay) Squadron before being given command of No. 121 (Eagle) Squadron in August. His tenure in this role would be brief, however, as, at the end of September, the squadron transferred to the USAAF. He moved to No. 124 (Baroda) Squadron as supernumerary squadron leader before being posted to India where he was posted to command No. 615 (County of Surrey) Squadron from January to May 1943. No further operational assignments followed before the end of the war.

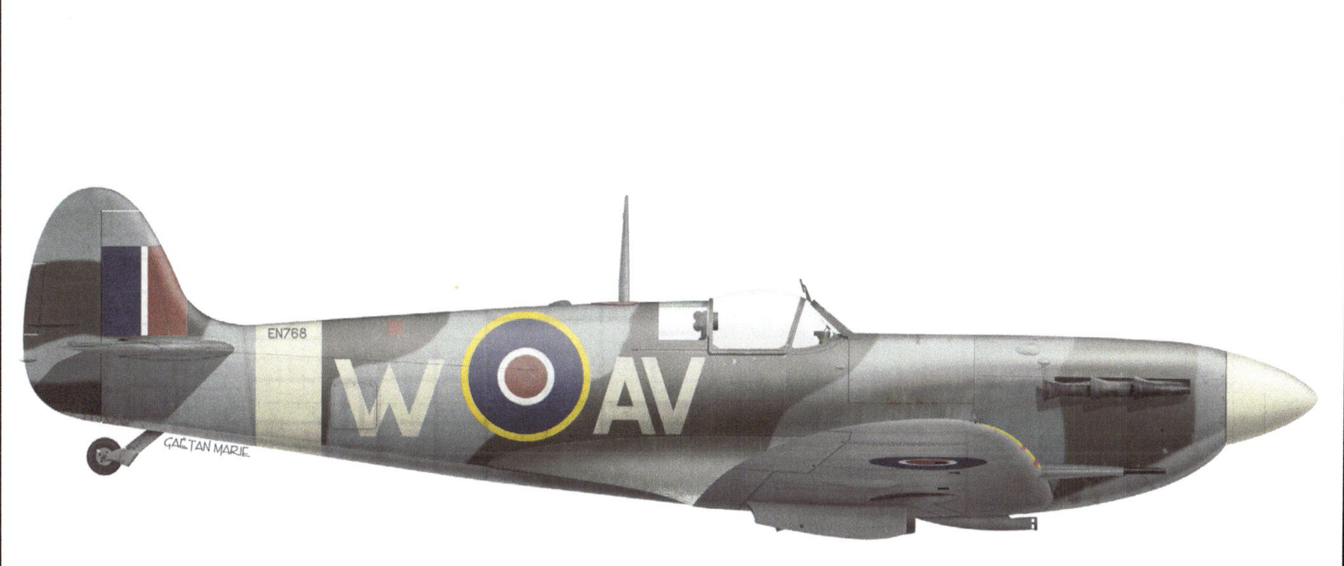

Supermarine Spitfire Mk VB EN798
No. 121 (Eagle) Squadron
Squadron Leader W.D. Williams
Southend (UK), September 1942

Date	Pilot	SN	Origin	Type	Serial	Code	Nb	Cat.
		HURRICANE MK II						
08.08.41	P/O Selden R. **EDNER**	RAF No. 64860	(US)/RAF	Ju88	**Z3427**	AV-R	0.5	P
	Sgt John J. **MOONEY**	CAN./ R.56127	(US)/RCAF		**Z5058**	AV-E	0.5	P
18.08.41	S/L Robin P.R. **POWELL**	RAF No. 33278	RAF	Bf109	**Z3493**		1.0	P
		SPITFIRE MK V						
23.03.42	P/O John J. **MOONEY**	CAN./ J.15024	(US)/RCAF	Fw190	**AA904**	AV-W	1.0	C
24.03.42	P/O Reade F. **TILLEY**	CAN./ J.15011	(US)/RCAF	Fw190	**AD463**		1.0	P
12.04.42	P/O LeRoy A. **SKINNER**	RAF No. 101460	(US)/RAF	Fw190	**AD501**		1.0	C
	F/L Thomas W. **ALLEN**	CAN./ J.15015	(US)/RCAF	Fw190	**BL986**	AV-T	1.0	P
15.04.42	P/O LeRoy A. **SKINNER**	RAF No. 101460	(US)/RAF	Fw190	**W3804**		1.0	C
	F/O Selden R. **EDNER**	RAF No. 64860	(US)/RAF	Fw190	**AA903**	AV-N	1.0	C
27.04.42	P/O William J. **DALEY**	RAF No. 101457	(US)/RAF	Ju52*	**P8794**	AV-Q	0.5	C
	P/O LeRoy A. **SKINNER**	RAF No. 101460	(US)/RAF		**W3804**		0.5	C
17.05.42	P/O William J. **DALEY**	RAF No. 101457	(US)/RAF	Fw190	**R6890**		1.0	C
	F/O Selden R. **EDNER**	RAF No. 64860	(US)/RAF	Fw190	**AA903**	AV-N	1.0	C
27.05.42	P/O William J. **DALEY**	RAF No. 101457	(US)/RAF	Bf109	**BL986**		1.0	C
08.06.42	F/L John J. **MOONEY**	CAN./ J.15024	(US)/RCAF	Fw190	**AD423**		2.0	C
	P/O Jackson B. **MAHON**	RAF No. 108640	(US)/RAF	Fw190	**?**		2.0	C
31.07.42	Sgt William P. **KELLY**	CAN./ R.89902	(US)/RCAF	Bf109	**BM581**	AV-P	1.0	C
	P/O Frank R. **BOYLES**	RAF No. 111571	(US)/RAF	Bf109	**AA841**		1.0	C
	F/L Selden R. **EDNER**	RAF No. 64860	(US)/RAF	Fw190	**EN918**	AV-X	2.0	C
	P/O Jackson B. **MAHON**	RAF No. 108640	(US)/RAF	Fw190	**BM405**	AV-J	2.0	C
	S/L Hugh C. **KENNARD**	RAF No. 40396	RAF	Bf109	**BL234**		1.0	C
19.08.42	Sgt Leon McF. **BLANDING**	CAN./ R.79288	(US)/RCAF	Fw190	**EN822**	AV-B	1.0	P
	F/L Selden R. **EDNER**	RAF No. 64860	(US)/RAF	Fw190	**EN918**	AV-X	1.0	C
	P/O Gilbert O. **HALSEY**	RAF No. 112619	(US)/RAF	Fw190	**BM590**	AV-R	1.0	P

Total: 26.0

**Actually a Junkers W34 but credited as a Ju52*

Two more pilots who scored while serving with 121:

Left, Reade Tilley from Florida. Frustrated by the British climate, and seeking more action, he chose to serve overseas and fought brilliantly with 126 Sqn over Malta during 1942. He returned to the UK in August 1942 with seven confirmed victories and a DFC. Two months later, he transferred to the USAAF but did not fly on operations again.

Right, 'Jim' Daley from Texas became the CO of the newly formed 335th FS when he transferred to the USAAF in September 1942. He was subsequently killed in a flying accident on 10.09.44 while serving with the P-47D-equipped 371st FG during his second European tour of operations.

Selden Raymond EDNER
RAF No. 64860

'Sel' Edner, from Minnesota, reported to the Clayton Knight Committee, which was recruiting American volunteers to serve in the RAF, in November 1940 and was accepted owing to his flying experience. In March 1941, after initial training in the USA, he sailed for England and attended 56 OTU. Upon completion, Edner was posted to No. 121 (Eagle) Squadron in June 1941, flying Hurricanes. Two months later, on 8 August, he shared in the probable destruction of a Ju88, his first claim, but it was on the Spitfire that Sel Edner would make the rest of his claims. Between 15 April and 19 August 1942, he filed seven more claims, bringing his scoreboard to five aircraft destroyed, one shared probable and two damaged. In September, he was awarded the DFC just before transferring to the USAAF. Later in the war, on 8 March 1944, he was shot down over Germany and became a PoW. Edner survived the war and served in Greece as part of the Military Assistance and Advisory Group during the civil war. Shot down while an observer in a light aircraft on 21 January 1949, he was subsequently captured and executed by his captors.

Supermarine Spitfire Mk VB EN918
No. 121 (Eagle) Squadron
Flight Lieutenant S.R. Edner
Southend (UK), August-September 1942

Jackson Barrett MAHON
RAF No. 108640

A Californian, 'Barry' Mahon joined the Eagles via the Clayton Knight Committee early in January 1941. Experienced, with nearly 300 hours of flight under his belt, he attended a refresher training course during the summer before sailing for the UK with a commission in the RAF. There, he attended 56 OTU and was posted to the second Eagle squadron, No. 121, in December. Mahon made his first claim on 12 April 1942 when he claimed an Fw190 damaged over the north of France. During the following weeks, he added further claims including two doubles in a single sortie for destroyed Fw190s on 8 June and 31 July, a unique achievement within the Eagles. On 19 August, he participated in Operation Jubilee over Dieppe, claiming an Fw190 destroyed and another probably destroyed. These would be his final claims as he was hit and baled out over the sea, sealing his tally at five confirmed victories, two probables and two damaged. He became an ace on that fateful day, one of five pilots to score the 'requisite' five kills while serving with the Eagle squadrons. Picked up by the Germans, he became a PoW, but was awarded the DFC in September.

Supermarine Spitfire Mk VB BM405
No. 121 (Eagle) Squadron
Pilot Officer J.B. Mahon
Southend (UK), June-July 1942

Date	Pilot	S/N	Origin	Serial	Code	Fate
			HURRICANE MK II			
02.10.41	F/Sgt Reade F. **TILLEY**	CAN./ R.64276	(US)/RCAF	**Z5058**	AV-E	-
			SPITFIRE MK V			
07.12.41	P/O Richard F. **PATTERSON**	CAN./ J.2928	(US)/RCAF	**W3711**	AV-H	†
12.12.41	P/O Kenneth LeR. **HOLDER**	RAF No. 118173	(US)/RAF	**AA871**	AV-D	†
08.03.42	P/O William L.C. **JONES**	CAN./ J.15052	(US)/RCAF	**AB206**	AV-S	†
09.03.42	P/O Roy W. **EVANS**	RAF No. 108632	(US)/RAF	**BL465**		-
24.03.42	P/O LeRoy A. **SKINNER**	RAF No. 101460	(US)/RAF	**BL963**		-
12.04.42	P/O Selden R. **EDNER**	RAF No. 64860	(US)/RAF	**BL447**		-
17.04.42	F/Sgt Frederick C. **AUSTIN**	CAN./ R.58580	(US)/RCAF	**AD498**	AV-C	†
25.04.42	P/O Bruce C. **DOWNS**	RAF No. 108631	(US)/RAF	**AB793**		-
28.04.42	P/O Carl G. **BODDING**	RAF No. 108628	(US)/RAF	**AD289**	AV-J	†
	P/O LeRoy A. **SKINNER**	RAF No. 101460	(US)/RAF	**W3804**		**PoW**
04.05.42	P/O Ralph W. **FREIBERG**	RAF No. 110340	(US)/RAF	**P8794**	AV-Q	†
	P/O Robert V. **BROSSMER**	RAF No. 106352	(US)/RAF	**AD460**	AV-P	†
31.05.42	F/L Thomas W. **ALLEN**	CAN./ J.15015	(US)/RCAF	**W3645**		†
16.06.42	F/L John J. **MOONEY**	CAN./ J.15024	(US)/RCAF	**W3841**		†
31.07.42	S/L Hugh C. **KENNARD**	RAF No. 40396	RAF	**BL234**		-
	P/O Norman D. **YOUNG**	RAF No. 116163	(US)/RAF	**AA732**		†
19.08.42	P/O James LaR. **TAYLOR**	RAF No. 110338	(US)/RAF	**AD569**		†
	P/O Jackson B. **MAHON**	RAF No. 108640	(US)/RAF	**BM405**	AV-J	**PoW**
	P/O Gene B. **FETROW**	RAF No. 113977	(US)/RAF	**BM401**	AV-P	-
	P/O Julian M. **OSBORNE**	RAF No. 112312	(US)/RAF	**P8589**		-
21.09.42	P/O John T. **SLATER***	RAF No. 116645	(US)/RAF	**P8339**	AV-I	†

As per 121 ORB, but Slater is officially a USAAF loss as O-885133, having made his transfer on 16 September but still wearing RAF uniform.

Total: 22

In conversation with HM King George VI, the A Flight CO, F/L A.W. Allen from South Carolina and P/O J.B. Jackson. Allen, was soon after posted missing in action on 31 May 1942 while Mahon became a PoW almost two months later.

Date	Pilot	S/N	Origin	Serial	Code	Fate
		HURRICANE MK I* & II				
15.06.41	P/O Richard F. **PATTERSON**	CAN./ J.2928	(US)/RCAF	**V7604***		-
21.06.41	P/O Loran L. **LAUGHLIN**	RAF No. 61925	(US)/RAF	**P3097***		†
27.07.41	P/O Warren V. **SHENK**	CAN./ J.15072	(US)/RCAF	**Z3317**		-
	Sgt Bradley **SMITH**	CAN./ R.67550	(US)/RCAF	**Z3422**		-
15.09.41	P/O Earl W. **MASON**	CAN./J.15009	(US)/RCAF	**Z3667**		†
		SPITFIRE MK V				
08.01.42	P/O Jack D. **GILLILAND**	RAF No. 106510	(US)/RAF	**W3240**	AV-X	†
23.06.42	P/O Julian M. **OSBORNE**	RAF No. 112312	(US)/RAF	**BL490**	AV-P	-

Total: 7

Richard F. Patterson from Virginia, in Hurricane Z3171/AV-B, wrecked the first 121 Sqn aircraft. Later on, in December 1941, he would also be the first of 121's pilots to be killed in action.

Victories - confirmed or probable claims: 24.5

Number of sorties: *ca.* 2,000

First operational sortie:
29.09.41
Last operational sortie:
26.09.42

Total aircraft written-off: 41

Aircraft lost on operations: 27
Aircraft lost in accidents: 14

Squadron code letters:
MD

COMMANDING OFFICERS				
S/L George A. Brown	RAF No. 39851	RAF	01.08.41	27.11.41
S/L Eric H. Thomas	RAF No. 39138	RAF	27.11.41	01.08.42
F/L Donald B.M. Blakeslee (*Temp.*)	Can./ J.4551	(us)/RCAF	01.08.42	01.09.42
S/L Caroll W. McColpin	RAF No. 61926	(us)/RAF	01.09.42	29.09.42

SQUADRON USAGE

The continuous flow of Americans enlisting in either the RAF or RCAF saw the formation of a third fighter unit, No. 133 Squadron, just ten weeks after the formation of the second 'Eagle' Squadron, 121. Formed at Coltishall on 1 August 1941, training immediately began on Hurricane Mk.IIs under the guidance of a British CO, S/L G.A. Brown, formerly of 71 Squadron. He was backed initially by his two flight commanders, also British, Flight Lieutenants H.A.S. Johnstone and G.W. Scott, who joined later on. The squadron re-located to Duxford on 15 August. Scott stayed for a short time before being posted to 601 Squadron at the beginning of September; his position was taken over by an American, F/L A. Mamedoff, posted in from 71 Squadron. He was one of the very few experienced American pilots to serve with 133 as, during August, new arrivals were all fresh graduates from No. 56 Operational Training Unit. Training progressed without major incidents until 27 September when Pilot Officers W.G. Soares and C.S. Barell collided while turning on approach to land. Both crashed at Anton Hill and were killed. Two days later, 133 became operational and, during the day, two scrambles were flown, as was a sweep over the North Sea. The next day, the squadron again flew patrols and a North Sea sweep. On 3 October, 133 moved to Fowlmere before moving to Eglington, the unit's new permanent base, on the 8th. The ferry flight turned into a dramatic event as fifteen Hurricanes were caught by bad weather and four pilots were killed (Pilot Officers W.J. White, R.N. Stout Jr and H.H. McCall, and the new B Flight CO, F/L Mamedoff. Mamedoff was replaced by another 71 Squadron pilot, F/L C.E. Bateman, who arrived on the 23rd. The squadron was withdrawn from service for a couple of days to recover from these sad losses. Operational activity resumed on the 14th. It was not long before the squadron suffered another accidental loss. On 23 October, P/O G.R. Bruce, a Canadian-born American, was returning from a convoy patrol when he made an unauthorised low pass over the airfield. Unfortunately, he struck a tree and crashed. Four days later, P/O J.G. Coxetter was killed when, during a navex, it is believed he entered cloud and lost control of his aircraft. He chose to abandon the Hurricane but did so too low; his chute did not have time to open properly. It was a sad month, even though the arrival of Spitfire IIs suggested a promising future. In November, 133 flew both types even though the Hurricanes began to be progressively withdrawn. December saw the last Hurricane sorties with a convoy patrol by Pilot Officers E. Doorly and C.A. Cook. With a new commander, S/L E.H. Thomas, who had taken over on 27 November, the squadron was ready to make another start. About 100 sorties were flown on Hurricanes by 133 Squadron. Soon after, on 30 November, GP/O R.L. Wolfe got lost in bad weather due to radio failure, ran out of fuel and baled out over the Irish Free State, being interned. He later escaped towards the end of 1943, and transferred to the USAAF in November of that year.

The squadron moved at Kirton-in-Lindsey early in January 1942 where 133 was re-equipped with the Spitfire Mk.VA, making it, therefore, one of the very few operational units to be fully equipped with this early version of the Mk.V. The first sorties, uneventful convoy patrols, were carried out on 6 January. Besides a handful of uneventful scrambles or dusk patrols, convoy patrols were the norm for the squadron in January. No flying could be performed during the first four days of February due to a continuous snowfall. Operational

George Alfred BROWN
RAF NO. 39851

George Brown joined the RAF on a short service commission in April 1937. At the outbreak of the war he was serving with No. 66 Squadron with which he would make his two claims, one confirmed Ju87 and another unconfirmed over Rotterdam on 13 May. Soon after, he was posted to No. 253 Squadron and participated in the Battle of Britain until being wounded in action on 30 August. He recovered from his injuries and was posted to the newly formed No. 71 (Eagle) Squadron - the first American-manned fighter unit - as a Flight commander. He remained with 71 until August 1941 when he was chosen to lead the third and last 'Eagle' squadron, No. 133 (Eagle) Squadron, then under formation and to bring the new pilots up to operational standard. He left the unit in November for a staff appointment at HQ Fighter Command and was awarded the DFC the following month. For his second tour of operations he was given command of No. 257 (Burma) Squadron, flying Typhoons, and led the unit until the end of his tour in April 1943. No more operational postings followed and he served in the Middle East until the end of war where he could be found commanding RAF Nicosia. He continued his career in the RAF after the war.

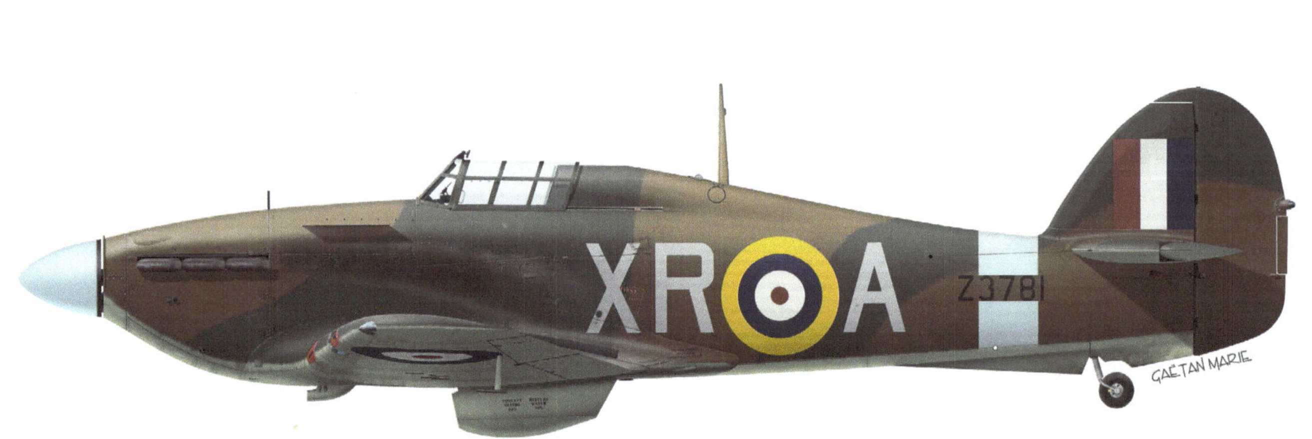

Hawker Hurricane Mk IIB Z3781
No. 133 (Eagle) Squadron
Flight Lieutenant G.A. Brown
North Weald (UK), spring 1941

Eric Hugh THOMAS
RAF No. 39138

Eric Thomas joined the RAF on a short service commission in July 1936 and served with No. 19 Squadron before the war. When the war broke out he was a flying instructor at the RAF College. As the need for fighter pilots became crucial in the summer of 1940, he returned to No. 19 Squadron on 19 August but was soon sent to No. 266 Squadron and then joined No. 222 (Natal) Squadron on 10 September. It is with the latter unit that he made his first claim, a shared Do17 destroyed, on the 15th. In October, he became a flight commander and remained with 222 until June 1941 when he was posted to No. 611 (County of Lancashire) Squadron as OC. At that time he had almost gained the status of ace with eight claims including four aircraft destroyed. In November that year, he was given commend of the third American-manned fighter unit of the RAF, No. 133 (eagle) Squadron, and was awarded the DFC. He was promoted to Wing Commander in August 1942 and posted to become WingCo of the Biggin Hill Wing. Before the end of the month, however, he was sent to the Hornchurch Wing. The following month, he received a Bar to his DFC and, on 9 October, he made his last claim, an Fw190 damaged. His score had risen to five confirmed victories (one shared), two probables (one shared) and five damaged aircraft. He left the Wing in November 1942 and was awarded the DSO in February 1943. Thomas relinquished his commission in September 1944 on account of ill-health.

Supermarine Spitfire Mk.VB BM263
No. 133 (Eagle) Squadron
Squadron Leader E.H. Thomas
Kirton-in-Lindsey (UK), spring 1942

Top and below, the CO's aircraft MD-A/BM263. Note the wheels painted with the RAF roundel and the unusual positioning of the squadron leader's pennant under the nose.

activity resumed on 5 February and the first combats ever for the squadron took place that day. The first involved a Ju88 sighted by F/L Johnstone at 09.30 while he was up conducting a weather test. The Junkers was flying north up the coast ten miles north of Spurn Head. Johnstone started to chase it, but the Junkers disappeared into cloud and was lost. The day wasn't over yet, however. In the afternoon, the squadron carried out its regular convoy patrols. In the middle of the afternoon, Johnstone and his number two, P/O M.A. Jackson from Texas, and F/L McColpin (who had recently taken over B Flight) teamed with Sgt W.C. Wicker (RCAF) from Illinois, were 45 minutes into their patrol when they spotted three Dornier 217s trying to bomb the convoy. The Dorniers were attacked by the 133 Squadron pilots, but also by other fighters from the escort, in this case, the Hurricanes of No. 253 Squadron. One Dornier was quickly accounted for and seen to crash by the escort vessel at the rear of the convoy. The victory was shared by Johnstone and Jackson, but also with two pilots of 253 Squadron. 'Red' McColpin returned to base with his guns empty and a report for a damaged Do217 to fill in. However, in the meantime, the squadron lost one of its Spitfires during a training flight when F/Sgt F.C. Austin (RCAF), an American from California, hit a snowdrift on take off. The Spitfire was too damaged to consider for repair. The rest of the month consisted of patrols and a few scrambles, but nothing really happened for the unit after the 5th. In all, the squadron carried out 306 sorties in February, its best total since formation. This total included some sorties flown by Spitfire VBs (aircraft borrowed from other units at Kirton and not officially allocated).

In March, uneventful convoy patrols basically took up the entire month. However, March was marked by the loss of the first pilot flying a Spitfire V. On the 16th, P/O H.C. Brown, a Canadian-born American, took off at 08.25 with F/Sgt C.W Harp (RCAF) from Alabama for a weather test over the Channel to establish whether convoy patrols could be safely conducted. When at a spot fifteen miles east of Mablethorpe, Harp called up Brown to tell him that he was going to climb as visibility was practically nil. There was no answer and it was assumed that Brown had crashed into the sea at that moment or just before. In March, the number of sorties dropped to less than 200. For the first half of April, the squadron carried out the usual convoy patrols with, on some days, a constant patrol maintained throughout the day. In this period of time, there were no encounters with the enemy. On the rare occasion the squadron was called to scramble, either as a precaution for an incoming raid or to investigate unidentified aircraft, the intercepted aircraft proved to be friendly in each case. While flying these uneventful patrols, training continued. On 3 April, two Spitfires collided during a training flight. While both pilots managed to abandon their aircraft, the parachute of P/O S.F. Whedon, an American from Wisconsin, caught a strong gust of wind and caused him to lose his footing, fall backwards, and fatally strike his head on a rock. On 16 April, the squadron participated in two fighter sweeps, led by W/C Walker, with the two other squadrons of the Wing, Nos. 19 and 412 Squadrons. Both were uneventful. After a further couple of patrols, 133 returned to the offensive with the Wing on the 24th, but, once more, the Luftwaffe could not be found when the Wing swept the north coast of France and into Belgium. The next day, the first Spitfire VB was lost in an accident when the aircraft flown by Sgt G.E. Eichar (RCAF) from Iowa was hit by a wind gust on landing. It bounced, stalled and an undercarriage leg collapsed. The Spitfire was declared damaged beyond economic repair. The following day, the 26th, the squadron took part in two other Wing ops over the same area as previous sweeps. During the first one early in the afternoon, 133 saw enemy aircraft beyond the edge of their formation, but did not engage. Later in the afternoon, the Wing returned over the French coast and, over Boulogne, it was attacked by Fw190s. Flight Lieutenant McColpin managed to shoot down one of them, it was seen crashing into the sea, and, in the melee, the squadrons were split up. On 27 April, the squadron, part of the Wing with Nos. 616 and 412 Squadrons, left West Malling to make

BM260/MD-C was lost on 5 June 1942 with its pilot, P/O Hancock.

No.133 (Eagle) Squadron in June 1942:
Standing, from left to right: P/O L.T. Ryerson from New Hampshire (killed 26.09.42), P/O G.H. Middleton from Iowa (PoW 26.09.42), P/O R.N. Beaty from New York, F/O E.L. Miller from Oklahoma, P/O D.D. Gudmundsen from Idaho (killed 06.09.42), P/O D.E. Lambert from California, P/O D.S. Gentile from Ohio, P/O J.M. Emerson (Intelligence Officer), F/O F.J.S. Chapman (Doctor), F/O D.G. Stavely-Dick (Adjutant), F/Sgt G.E. Eichar from Iowa (killed 31.07.42), F/Sgt C.H. Robertson from Mississippi.
Front row, from left to right: P/O C.W. Harp from Alabama (killed 31.07.42), P/O W.A. Arends from North Dakota (killed 20.06.42), P/O G.I. Omens from Illinois (killed 26.07.42), P/O E.D. Taylor from Oklahoma, F/L C.C. King from Missouri (killed 31.07.42), S/L E.H. Thomas, F/L D.J.M. Blakeslee from Ohio, P/O G.B. Sperry from California (PoW 26.09.42), P/O E. Doorly from New Jersey, P/O K.K. Kimbro from Mississippi, P/O W.H. Baker from Texas (killed 26.09.42).

a rendezvous at Southend with the North Weald Wing. The Wing was acting as top cover with 133 flying high cover for *Circus* 142. On reaching Ostend, about thirty Fw190s were seen above at 21,000 feet. Blue Section was engaged by some of them when they dived and, in the ensuing melee, P/O R.L. Pewitt, from Texas, claimed one Fw190 as probably destroyed. At the same time White Section was attacked from below and P/O W.H. Baker, another Texan, chased a Fw190 down to 10,000 feet, firing a long burst. Baker also claimed it as probably destroyed. Shortly after this, the Wing turned for home and F/Sgt W.C. Wicker from Illinois was heard over the radio reporting that he had been hit. Posted missing on arrival at base, his body was washed up at Dover two days later. No more offensive operations were carried out before the end of the month, only regular patrols. On 29 April, the CO took off with P/O E. Doorly from New Jersey at 02.30 for a night patrol. They encountered a Do217 and it was engaged, Doorly claiming it as damaged. He was hit by return fire, however, probably in the glycol system as the engine temperature began to rise almost immediately and, before he could reach the coast, the engine stopped, forcing him to abandon the Spitfire six miles south-east of Church Fenton. He landed safely. April saw the squadron's real entry into the air war with the first combat with German fighters over the Continent producing encouraging results. The squadron was now fully equipped with the Mk.VB.

No operational flights were performed during the first days of May as the squadron was involved in its move to Biggin Hill which it completed on the 3rd. The first operation, a fighter sweep with the rest of the Wing (Nos. 72, 124 and 401 Squadrons), was carried out on the 7th. The squadron acted as top cover for six Bostons detailed to bomb Ostend. No enemy was seen and the op was conducted without incident. Two more sweeps were flown on the 9th, another on the 10th, and, again, all aircraft returned with nothing to report even though, on the raid on the 10th, the enemy was seen, but not engaged (the squadron ran into a bunch of Bf109s flying at 21,000 feet, but the chase was abandoned when the Germans put their noses down and dived away). On the 9th, 133 celebrated its one thousandth sortie since formation. It returned to the north coast of France one week later and this time luck was with the Eagles. The Luftwaffe accepted the engagement and, by the time it was over, F/L McColpin was able to fill in two claims for Bf109s (one confirmed and one probable) and P/O M.S. Morris, from Oklahoma, one probable. This was achieved without losses on the Eagles' side. The next day, the squadron was engaged by six German fighters over the Dieppe area. While the CO and Californian P/O G.B. Sperry were able to get into good firing positions, no claims were made. The result was totally different on the following day, the 19th. During another sweep over the Fécamp-Le Tréport area, the Luftwaffe intercepted the Wing and, in the ensuing combat, F/Sgt C.W. Harp, from Alabama, claimed two Fw190s destroyed, while P/O M.S. Morris from Oklahoma added a Bf109 destroyed and another damaged to his tally. Pilot Officer Sperry was also happy to return with a claim to fill in, a damaged Bf109, even though he would have to share it with the Biggin Hill Wing. Two pilots, however, did not make it home. Pilot Officer R.L. Pewitt from Texas was seen to go down with two fighters on his tail about ten miles south of Beachy Head. His aircraft was hit and severely damaged and he crashed into the sea off Beachy Head. He was rescued, but died of head injuries before being admitted to hospital. The other pilot posted missing, and believed to have been shot down, was P/O D.R. Florance, a Canadian-born American, whose body was never recovered. After a period of patrols, 133 returned, uneventfully as it turned out, to the offensive on the 23rd. The next day, Pilot Officers M.E. Jackson from Texas and E.D. Taylor from Oklahoma were patrolling off the Dungeness-Hastings area when they spotted two Bf109s returning to the French coast. They ran after them and Jackson closed in enough to be able to fire a short burst and damage one of the fleeing fighters. Later that day, the squadron was in action for another sweep over the Hardelot-Saint-Omer area, but, while many enemy aircraft was seen, it was unable to engage. Before the end of the month, 133 took part in six more sweeps over France and its tally increased with one Fw190 damaged on the 27th (S/L E.H. Thomas) and another, by P/O Taylor, on the 31st during the last sweep of the month. This latter claim was thin compensation for the loss of two pilots, P/O M.S. Morris and Texan P/O W.K. Ford, who were both shot down and killed by Fw190s. Pilot Officer Doorly's Spitfire was also damaged during the combat, but managed to get back to base.

In June, the squadron beat its record of number of sorties with 327, a figure that would not be surpassed before the transfer to the USAAF at the end of September. June was indeed busy. It started with three operations over France on the first day of the month (10.50, 12.50 and 17.50), but the Germans did not show up. Two more ops were carried out the next day and on the 3rd without incident. On the 4th, in the very early hours of the day, the squadron flew as air cover at 4000 feet for commandos making a raid on a RDF station inland of Plage-Ste-Cecile before withdrawing. Two Bf109s made an attempt to attack from behind, but the squadron turned into them and forced the German fighters to turn away. The following day, the squadron was back over Abbeville in France for a diversionary sweep with No. 72 Squadron. The Germans took off and engaged the Spitfires. The combat was rather balanced as the CO claimed one Fw190 as probably destroyed, but Californian P/O F. Hancock was posted missing. Up to the 20th, operational activity decreased owing mainly to bad weather. In this period of time, only three offensive ops were flown alongside some routine patrols. On the 20th, the squadron participated in another diversionary sweep over the Hardelot-Saint-Omer area while Bostons were bombing Le Havre. The Germans intercepted the squadron to their advantage, caught the last section of the formation and shot down P/O W. Arends from North Dakota. Another sweep to Dunkirk was conducted on the 23rd without incident and, on the 24th, eight aircraft were sent on a convoy patrol from 05.00 hours. Two aircraft scrambled at 06.55, over Rye and Dungeness, to 20,000 feet. Pilot Officers G.I. Omens, from Illinois, and W.C. Slade, from Texas, saw a He111 escorted by three Bf109s, but the Eagles were unable to intercept. Before the end of the month, the squadron participated in another two sweeps over France, but no incidents were reported. However, in the same period to time, some patrols were flown and on the 27th, while patrolling Tenterden at 28,000 feet, F/L D.L.M. Blakselee, the new B Flight CO, and P/O C.W. Harp from Alabama saw a Ju88 flying below at 27,500 feet. They chased it back to Boulogne and although they fired all their cannon rounds, neither was able to get within 400 yards and no claim was filed. Later on, Blakeslee filed a report for a Ju88 damaged. On the last day of June, the squadron made a move to Lympne.

The first week of July was spent flying uneventful patrols. It was not until the 7th that the squadron returned to France when A Flight escorted Hurribombers over Fécamp in company with a flight from No. 234 Squadron. This was the only major action flown from Lympne and the unit returned to Biggin Hill a few days later. July 12 was a busy day with constant patrols flown between 05.10 and 09.15 before the squadron took part in a fighter sweep over the French coast around midday. Later that day it acted as escort cover, with the rest of the Wing, for Bostons bombing Abbeville aerodrome. More ops were flown over the Continent during the next few days, including the first mass Rhubarb, from 20 July. The end of July was approaching and, despite a lot of sorties, no combats were experienced to change the routine. Sadly, this routine was broken on the 28th when P/O B.P. deHaven from Kentucky was killed a flying accident. The reasons for the crash would never be clearly established. Eventually, what the Eagle pilots were looking for, dogfights with the Luftwaffe, occurred on the 31st during the day's first sweep over France early in the afternoon. They were escorting twelve Bostons targeting Abbeville aerodrome once more and 133 was flying with Nos. 65 and 72 Squadrons. The unit was acting as close escort to the Bostons, flying at 8000 feet, which bombed the aerodrome without incident. However, just before reaching the coast on the way back, a number of Fw190s appeared and a fierce melee ensued. Two confirmed victories were claimed in sequence by P/O W.H.

Mid-June 1942 at Biggin Hill: F/Sgt C.H. Robertson from Mississippi, a new comer, P/O W.A. Arends from North Dakota, P/O C.A. Cook from California, P/O E.D. Taylor from Oklahoma, F/L D.J.M. Blakeslee. A few days after this photo was taken, Arends was killed in action (20.06.42). Taylor was wounded in action the following month on 31 July and was taken to an hospital. He never returned to 133 and eventually transferred to the USAAF in October 1942.

Don Blakeslee about to taxi EN851/MD-U out for another op during the summer of 1942. He would make several claims while flying this aircraft.

Baker and P/O E.D. Taylor (Oklahoma), the latter also claiming a damaged Bf109. However, the squadron's casualties were not light. A Flight lost F/L C.C. King from Missouri, P/O C.W. Harp and F/Sgt G.E. Eichar (RCAF) from Iowa. All were shot down and killed and Taylor was put out of action, injured and taken to an hospital; he never returned to 133. The same day, the squadron went to Gravesend where it remained before returning to Lympne on 17 August.

On 1 August, 133 flew its first operation from Gravesend, an escort for six Bostons bombing Bruges in Belgium. It was an uneventful way to start the month and all aircraft returned safely. Convoy patrols were flown over the next few days before the squadron was sent on an anti-shipping sweep off Boulogne and Le Havre on the 5th. No ships were seen. That day, temporary command was given to F/L Blakeslee as S/L Thomas had been promoted to Wing Commander and left to become wing leader of the Biggin Hill Wing. The next day, 133 participated in another sweep over the Belgian coast, escorting the 307th Fighter Squadron's (FS) Spitfires. An uneventful *Rodeo* was flown on the 9th and no further sorties were followed until the 15th. Having returned to Lympne, the squadron escorted twelve B-17 Flying Fortresses to Rouen, the first mission by these bombers over the European continent. On the 18th, with 65 Squadron and the USAAF's 307th FS, the unit flew another *Rodeo* to Dunkirk. They made a wide detour inland from Dunkirk and were just inland of Sangatte when they were attacked by about ten Fw190s. Led by F/L Blakeslee, the squadron made a 360 degree orbit, turning inside a couple of the Fw190s which allowed Blakeslee to give one a good burst. Plenty of cannon shells hit the enemy aircraft and the German pilot abandoned his fatally hit aircraft. The remaining enemy aircraft disappeared and no further combat took place. All of the Spitfires returned to base safely. On 19 August, Operation *Jubilee* was launched. The RAF had to play an important role in supporting the various naval and army elements. As far as 133 Squadron was concerned, four patrols were carried out – 0720-0840, 1015-1130, 1225-1345 and 1955-2055. On the first patrol, led by Blakeslee, the squadron was tasked with orbiting over Dieppe at 7,000 feet shortly before 08.00. Soon after they arrived over the target, the enemy appeared. In the ensuing melee, Blakeslee and P/O W.H. Baker shot down one Fw190 each while F/Sgt R.L. Alexander from Illinois opened his score by claiming a probable Fw190. The squadron suffered no casualties. The second patrol also led to furious combats. This time, 133 was required to fly at 12,000 feet over Dieppe. Combat commenced immediately the target was reached. As the Americans turned for home, no less than two Fw190s, one Ju88, and one Do217 were claimed as destroyed, the victorious pilots being F/L E.G. Bretell, a British pilot recently posted in as a flight commander to replace F/L King (killed on 31 July), F/L Blakeslee, and P/O D.S. Gentile from Ohio who claimed the Ju88 and a Fw190. A number of other pilots also made claims: New Yorker P/O R.N. Beaty with a Do217 and a Fw190 damaged, F/L Blakeslee, P/O W.H. Baker and P/O G.G. Wright from Pennsylvania each claimed a Fw190 damaged, as well P/O D.D. Gudmunsden from Idaho, who was flying an American Spitfire (307th FS/MX-K), and P/O Doorly and Bretell also damaged a Do217 each. The harvest of claims was not over and during the third patrol, F/Sgt R.L. Alexander added a Do217 destroyed while F/L Blakeslee and F/O J.C. Nelson from Colorado claimed a damaged Fw190 and Do217 respectively. That was, without a doubt, the day of fame for the squadron as it made all of these claims without loss.

The next day, 133 carried out a *Rodeo* over Saint-Omer as a diversionary sweep. No combat was reported. Within days of Operation *Jubilee*, No. 133 Squadron moved to Martlesham Heath where it undertook a nine-day conversion to the latest Spitfire variant, the Mk.IX. At the time, this mark had just started its career with the RAF, in June with No. 64 Squadron, and the selection of an Eagle squadron could be seen as a hint for the future with all three Eagle squadrons now planned for transfer to the USAAF at the end of September equipped with the new mark. The squadron was the fifth to be converted. On 30 August, 133 moved back to Biggin Hill with the brand new Mk.IXs under the command of a new CO, S/L 'Red' McColpin, who had previously served with No. 71 Squadron.

Continuing to use a handful of Mk.Vs for training, one was lost during a practice flight on 19 September, killing New Yorker Pilot Officer S.M. Schwatzberg.

The first Mk.IX sorties were carried out on 4 September when Pilot Officers E.D. Beatty and L.T. Ryerson scrambled and were ordered to orbit over Canterbury as a high-flying intruder had been detected. The pair continued to climb and eventually sighted a Ju86R heading south-west over North Foreland. The Junkers was climbing through 40,000 feet when Beatty closed on it; positioned slightly astern and below, he opened fire with a short burst of cannons and machine guns. He reported seeing strikes on the underside. At that moment, Beatty's Spitfire faltered at the extreme altitude and he was forced to descend. As he passed 20,000 feet, the engine caught fire and Beatty was forced to bale out, landing in the sea east of Manston. He was picked up and filed a claim report for an enemy aircraft damaged. Two days later, 133 was airborne for its first escort tasking with the Mk.IX, being part of an escort for 36 B-17 Flying Fortresses heading to Abbeville. The formation was intercepted by German fighters and the squadron was involved in an air combat near Méaulte. Flying Officer E Doorly shot down an Fw190 before being hit and baling out. He survived and managed to evade to eventually return to England in March 1943 where he finally filed his combat report. Pilot Officer R.D. Gudmundsen was less fortunate and was killed, possibly by inexperienced B-17 gunners who opened fire on their escort. The following day, the squadron, led by F/L Gordon Brettell, an Englishman, formed part of the escort for a B-17 mission to the shipyards at Rotterdam that, coming off target, was intercepted by a small formation of Fw190s. One was chased by P/O W.H. Baker who soon got into a perfect position, firing several accurate bursts. It was not seen to crash and therefore was only credited as a probable. This was to be one of the last main actions for some time as the Americans were preoccupied with their pending USAAF transfer and all the administration that entailed. However, some patrols were flown. During one of these, in the early hours of 16 September, P/O C.H. Miley spotted a pair of Fw190s over the sea east of Deal. He promptly turned west and gave chase, firing a long burst at the lead aircraft as it turned towards him. It was hit and headed away trailing smoke. Baker was credited with a damaged.

On 26 September, 133 was tasked with escorting B-17s from the 97th Bomb Group to attack an aircraft repair facility and adjacent railways at Morlaix on the north coast of Brittany. The Americans were part of a formation comprising Nos. 401 (RCAF) and 64 Squadrons, both also flying the Mk.IX; 133 was to act as close cover with 401, 64 as top cover. The wing leader, W/C Brian Kingcome, was absent for this op, so 64 Squadron's CO, the Australian S/L 'Tony' Gaze, assumed the role. The raid had been postponed several times due to bad weather while 133 was preparing to transfer to the USAAF. For this purpose, 133 moved to Great Sampford, a satellite of Duxford, on the 23rd. Also absent was 133's CO, S/L McColpin, who had been ordered to London for meetings; his senior flight commander, F/L Brettell, led the unit. While the raid went ahead on the 26th, the weather still proved problematic. Take-off was made without incident, but the fighters of the wing missed the rendezvous with the bombers. Thinking the fighters had arrived early (the B-17s were actually ahead, continuing their course), S/L Gaze ordered the rest of the wing to circle and head towards Brittany, calling for fixes but getting no response. At the same time, the formation was pushed off course by an unexpected powerful high-altitude wind, what is now known as the Jetstream. Problems began to arise for the pilots of 133 Squadron. After about 50 minutes of flight, P/O G.P. Neville from Oklahoma saw his engine begin developing trouble and was ordered to return to base escorted by P/O R.N. Beaty from New York City. Owing to the bad weather, and thinking they were now over the British soil, they descended and broke cloud. They were still over Brittany and, attempting to land at an airfield near Guingamp, encountered flak; Neville was shot down and killed. Beaty managed to escape, heading north and crossing the Channel before running out of fuel near Kingsbridge where he crash-landed, seriously injuring himself in the process.

In the meantime, the remaining ten Spitfires continued their flight but, after two hours and now heading north with the wing, fuel levels began to create concern among the pilots. At that moment, a hole in the overcast was seen by P/O Baker from Texas; F/L Brettell agreed to let him go down to investigate. A misunderstanding saw the whole squadron follow Baker as the other two squadrons watched in amazement. Now totally on their own, the pilots of 133 broke through the overcast into poor weather. They found a town they thought to be Plymouth or Southampton and flew towards it, looking for a place to land before running out of fuel. It was not Plymouth or Southampton, but the very well-defended harbour of Brest in Brittany. Flak soon opened up and, helped by a few Fw190s which had scrambled in response to the Spitfires, caused carnage. A short dogfight took place with some of the Eagle pilots; F/L M.E. Jackson, another Texan, managed to shoot one of the Fw190s down, claiming the final victory for an Eagle squadron. He soon fell victim to another Fw190, however, and crash landed to become a PoW, albeit badly injured (his claim would be filed after the war). He was not the only one of the formation to become a PoW. The others were: F/L Brettell, who was also injured; F/O G.B. Sperry from California; P/O C.A. Cook, also from California; and Pilot Officers G.H. Middleton from Iowa and G.G. Wright from Pennsylvania (although Wright evaded for six weeks). Despite officially being USAAF officers for a couple of days, all of them were still wearing RAF uniforms, so were sent to an RAF PoW camp. Others were less fortunate and lost their lives: F/O W.H. Baker Jr from Texas; P/O L.T. Ryerson from New Hampshire; and P/O D.D. Smith from Oklahoma. Only P/O R.E. Smith from Maryland managed to evade capture and eventually return to England in March 1943. The operation was one of the worst disasters experienced by an RAF fighter unit during WW2.

The squadron was hurriedly re-equipped with Spitfire Mk.Vs as the RAF did not have enough Mk.IXs at the time to replace such substantial losses. It was also the easiest way for 133 to get some aircraft before the official transfer ceremony to the USAAF on the 29th as 336th FS of the 4th FG.

Date	Pilot	SN	Origin	Type	Serial	Code	Nb	Cat.
		SPITFIRE MK V						
05.02.42	F/L Hugh A.S. **JOHNSTONE**	RAF No. 88723	RAF	Do217	**P8195**	MD-X	0.25	C*
	P/O Marion E. **JACKSON**	RAF No. 100519	(US)/RAF		**P9397**		0.25	C*
26.04.42	F/L Caroll W. **McCOLPIN**	RAF No. 61926	(US)/RAF	Fw190	**BM300**		1.0	C
27.04.42	P/O Robert L. **PEWITT**	RAF No. 100528	(US)/RAF	Fw190	**BL988**		1.0	P
	P/O William H. **BAKER**	RAF No. 108826	(US)/RAF	Fw190	**BL492**		1.0	P
17.05.42	P/O Moran S. **MORRIS**	RAF No. 102052	(US)/RAF	Bf109	**BL996**		1.0	P
	F/L Caroll W. **McCOLPIN**	RAF No. 61926	(US)/RAF	Bf109	**BM300**		1.0	C
	F/L Caroll W. **McCOLPIN**	RAF No. 61926	(US)/RAF	Bf109	**BM300**		1.0	P
19.05.42	P/O Moran S. **MORRIS**	RAF No. 105052	(US)/RAF	Bf109	**BL996**		1.0	C
	F/Sgt Carter W. **HARP**	CAN./ R.74201	(US)/RCAF	Bf109	**BL982**		2.0	C
05.06.42	S/L Eric H. **THOMAS**	RAF No. 39138	RAF	Bf109	**BM263**	MD-A	1.0	P
31.07.42	P/O William H. **BAKER**	RAF No. 108826	(US)/RAF	Fw190	**EN924**	MD-J	1.0	C
	P/O Edwin D. **TAYLOR**	RAF No. 102053	(US)/RAF	Fw190	**BM591**		1.0	C
18.08.42	F/L Donald J.M. **BLAKESLEE**	CAN./ J.4551	(US)/RCAF	Bf109	**EN951**	MD-U	1.0	C
19.08.42	F/Sgt Richard L. **ALEXANDER**	CAN./ R.67881	(US)/RCAF	Fw190	**BL773**		1.0	P
	F/L Donald J.M. **BLAKESLEE**	CAN./ J.4551	(US)/RCAF	Fw190	**EN951**	MD-U	1.0	P
	P/O William H. **BAKER**	RAF No. 108826	(US)/RAF	Fw190	**EN834**	MD-D	1.0	C
	F/L Edward G. **BRETELL**	RAF No. 61053	RAF	Fw190	**AD237**		1.0	C
	F/L Donald J.M. **BLAKESLEE**	CAN./ J.4551	(US)/RCAF	Do217	**EN951**	MD-U	1.0	C
	P/O Dominic S. **GENTILE**	RAF No. 112302	(US)/RAF	Fw190	**BM530**	MD-C	1.0	C
				Ju88	**BM530**	MD-C	1.0	C
	F/Sgt Richard L. **ALEXANDER**	CAN./ R.67881	(US)/RCAF	Do217	**AB910**		1.0	C

Shared with two No.253 Sqn pilots, P/O P. Landers and Sgt J.C. Tate.

Date	Pilot	SN	Origin	Type	Serial	Code	Nb	Cat.
		SPITFIRE MK IX						
06.09.42	F/O Eric **DOORLY**	RAF No. 101458	(US)/RAF	Fw190	**BS276**		1.0	C
07.09.42	P/O William H. **BAKER**	RAF No. 108826	(US)/RAF	Fw190	**BS137**	MD-D	1.0	P
26.09.42	F/L Marion E. **JACKSON**	RAF No. 100519	(US)/RAF	Fw190	**BS279**		1.0	C

Total: 24.5

Without doubt Dominic 'Don' Gentile has been one of the most outstanding pilots who joined 133 Sqn. Born in Ohio he enlisted in the RAF in 1941 and after his commission, he sailed from Halifax (Canada) to the United Kingdom in December that year. There, he learned to fly Spitfires and he reported to the Squadron early in June 1942. He distinguished himself during Operation 'Jubilee', during which he claimed two confirmed victories. The following month, he transferred to the US Army Air Force and continued to fly with the 4th FG flying Spitfires then P-47 Thunderbolts. But what will make Gentile famous began when he made the transition from the P-47 to the P-51 Mustang. Between December 1943 and April 1944, he managed to claim 22 German aircraft as destroyed to become one the top aces of the USAAF. In April 1944 he was sent back to the USA and never flew in operations again. He left the Army in 1946 but soon re-entered the new US Air Force in December 1947. Sadly, he was killed on 28 January 1951 during a routine training flight on a T-33.

Donald James Matthew BLAKESLEE
CAN/ J.4551

An American from Ohio, Don Blakeslee enlisted in the RCAF in August 1940. Having some flying experience, his initial training was shorter than the norm and, in April 1941, he sailed for England, where he completed his training. before being posted to No. 411 (RCAF) Squadron in June, prior to a move to No. 401 (RCAF) Squadron in October. He opened his score on 18 November by claiming a Bf109 as damaged over Berck in France. Other claims followed until June 1942 when he was posted to No. 133 (Eagle) Squadron as a flight commander. During the summer, he continued to score until 19 August when, over Dieppe, he made his last claim for the RCAF and was awarded the DFC the same month. At the end of September, he was transferred to the USAAF, where he continued to fly operationally and add to his personal tally. During the summer of 1944, he was OC of the 4th Fighter Group; in this role he made his final claim on 2 July. He left the group in October, but no further operational positions followed. He remained with the USAAF after the war.

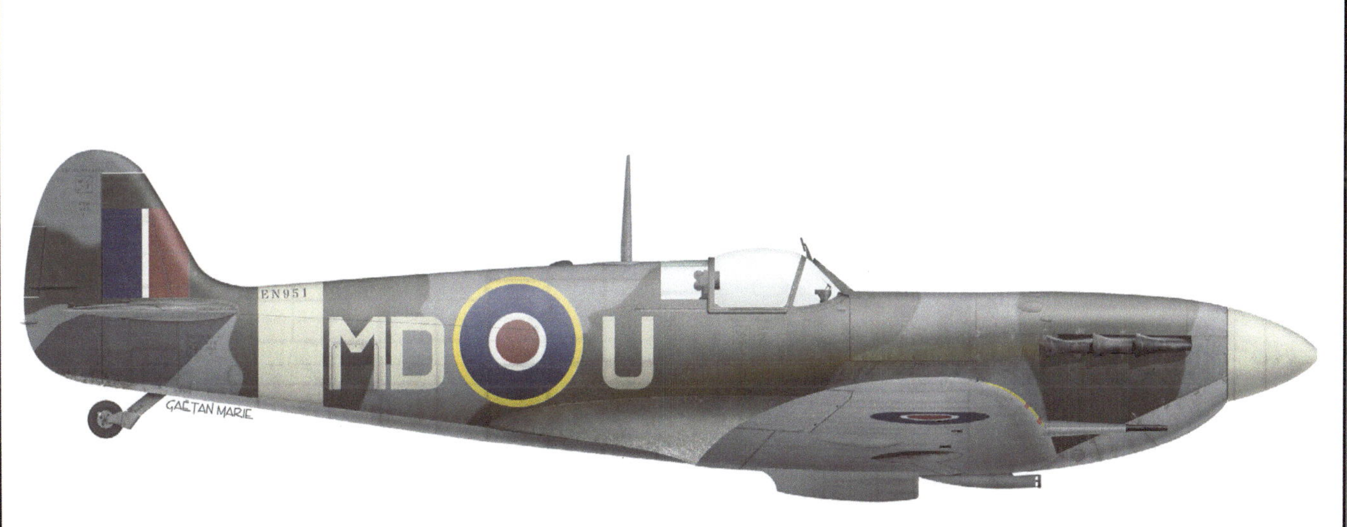

Supermarine Spitfire Mk.VB EN951
No. 133 (Eagle) Squadron
Flight Lieutenant D.J.M. Blakeslee
Gravesend (UK), August 1942

Date	Pilot	S/N	Origin	Serial	Code	Fate
		HURRICANE MK II				
23.10.41	P/O George R. **BRUCE**	RAF No. 67580	(US)/RAF	**Z3649**		†
		SPITFIRE MK V				
16.03.42	P/O Hugh C. **BROWN**	RAF No. 103467	(US)/RAF	**X4353**		†
27.04.42	F/Sgt Walter C. **WICKER**	CAN./ R.74415	(US)/RCAF	**BM264**		†
29.04.42	P/O Eric **DOORLY**	RAF No. 101458	(US)/RAF	**BL995**	MD-G	-
19.05.42	P/O Robert L. **PEWITT**	RAF No. 100528	(US)/RAF	**BL988**		†
	P/O David R. **FLORANCE**	CAN./ J.15193	(US)/RCAF	**AD502**		†
31.05.42	P/O William K. **FORD**	RAF No. 111238	(US)/RAF	**BL961**		†
	P/O Moran S. **MORRIS**	RAF No. 102052	(US)/RAF	**BL996**		†
05.06.42	P/O Fletcher **HANCOCK**	RAF No. 112280	(US)/RAF	**BM260**	MD-C	†
20.06.42	P/O William A. **ARENDS**	RAF No. 112280	(US)/RAF	**EP168**		†
31.07.42	F/L Coburn C. **KING**	RAF No. 100521	(US)/RAF	**BL938**		†
	P/O Carter W. **HARP**	CAN./ J.15389	(US)/RCAF	**BL982**		†
	F/Sgt Grant E. **EICHAR**	CAN./ R.83097	(US)/RCAF	**BM646**		†
		SPITFIRE MK IX				
04.09.42	P/O Ernest D. **BEATY**	RAF No. 116468	(US)/RAF	**BS297**		-
06.09.42	P/O Dick D. **GUDMUNDSEN**	RAF No. 112295	(US)/RAF	**BS292**	MD-K	†
	F/O Eric **DOORLY**	RAF No. 101458	(US)/RAF	**BS276**		Eva.
26.09.42	F/L Edward G. **BRETTEL**	RAF No. 61053	RAF	**BS313**	MD-A	PoW
	F/L Marion E. **JACKSON**	RAF No. 100519	(US)/RAF	**BS279**		PoW
	F/O George B. **SPERRY**	RAF No. 100533	(US)/RAF	**BS446**		PoW
	P/O Charles A. **COOK**	RAF No. 103476	(US)/RAF	**BS138**		PoW
	P/O George H. **MIDDLETON**	RAF No. 112311	(US)/RAF	**BS301**		PoW
	P/O Gilbert G. **WRIGHT**	RAF No. 112286	(US)/RAF	**BR638**	MD-F	PoW
	P/O Gene P. **NEVILLE***	RAF No. 115120	(US)/RAF	**BS294**	MD-I	†
	P/O Leonard T. **RYERSON***	RAF No. 112285	(US)/RAF	**BS140**	MD-M	†
	F/O William H. **BAKER** JR.*	RAF No. 108626	(US)/RAF	**BS275**		†
	P/O Dennis D. **SMITH***	RAF No. 116464	(US)/RAF	**BS447**		†
	P/O Robert E. **SMITH**	RAF No.116463	(US)/RAF	**BR640**	MD-V	Eva.

As per 133 ORB, but they are all officially a USAAF losses as respectivelly O-885129, O-885137, O-885113, O-885128, having made their transfer but still wearing RAF uniform.

Total: 27

William A. Arends, from North Dakota, just before he was shot down and killed by Fw190s on 20 June 1942. He had joined 133 Sqn the previous March. He's posing on the wing of his Spitfire, EP168.

Summary of the aircraft lost by accident - 133 (Eagle) Squadron

Date	Pilot	S/N	Origin	Serial	Code	Fate
		HURRICANE MK II				
27.09.41	P/O Walter G. **SOARES**	RAF No. 100532	(US)/RAF	**Z3335**	MD-B	†
	P/O Charles S. **BARRELL**	RAF No. 102519	(US)/RAF	**Z3828**	MD-F	†
08.10.41	F/L Andrew B. **MAMEDOFF**	RAF No. 81621	(US)/RAF	**Z3781**	MD-U	†
	P/O William J. **WHITE**	RAF No. 100535	(US)/RAF	**Z3457**	MD-Y	†
	P/O Roy N. **STOUT** Jr.	RAF No. 100531	(US)/RAF	**Z3253**		†
	P/O Hugh H. **MCCALL**	RAF No. 67583	(US)/RAF	**Z3677**		†
27.10.41	P/O James G. **COXETTER**	RAF No. 104392	(US)/RAF	**Z3182**		†
		SPITFIRE MK II				
30.11.41	P/O Roland L. **WOLFE**	RAF No. 102518	(US)/RAF	**P8074**		Int.
		SPITFIRE MK V				
05.02.42	F/Sgt Frederick C. **AUSTIN**	CAN./ R.58580	(US)/RCAF	**W3379**		-
03.04.42	P/O Samuel F. **WHEDON**	RAF No. 101462	(US)/RAF	**P8438**		†
	P/O William A. **ARENDS**	RAF No. 112280	(US)/RAF	**P8595**		-
25.04.42	Sgt Grant E. **EICHAR**	CAN./ R.83097	(US)/RCAF	**BL967**		-
28.07.42	P/O Ben P. **DEHAVEN**	RAF No. 116467	(US)/RAF	**BL807**		†
19.09.42	P/O Seymour M. **SCHATZBERG**	RAF No. 118585	(US)/RAF	**EP167**	MD-H	†

Total: 14

Supermarine Spitfire Mk.VB AB875
No. 71 (Eagle) Squadron
Martlesham Heath (UK), February 1942

Supermarine Spitfire Mk.VB AD196
No. 71 (Eagle) Squadron
Martlesham Heath (UK), February 1942

Supermarine Spitfire Mk.VB BL287
No. 71 (Eagle) Squadron
Martlesham Heath (UK), March 1942

Supermarine Spitfire Mk.VB W3711
No. 121 (Eagle) Squadron
Kirton-in-Lindsey (UK), December 1941

SQUADRONS! - The series

Donald James Matthew BLAKESLEE DFC

Supermarine Spitfire Mk.VB EN951
No. 133 (Eagle) Squadron
Flight Lieutenant D. J. M. Blakeslee
USA / J 4351
Gravesend (UK), August 1942

Charles Cuthbertson LEARMONTH DFC*

Douglas Boston Mk. III A28-9 (ex-AL811)
No. 22 Squadron RAAF
Squadron Leader C. C. Learmonth
A4391
Port Moresby (New Guinea), spring 1943

Hans Anton MAURENBRECHER

Curtiss P-40N-35-CU C3-560
No. 120 (NEI) Squadron
Major H. Maurenbrecher
Biak (New Guinea), 1945-1946

Roland Prosper BEAMONT DSO* DFC*

Hawker Tempest Mk.V JN751
No. 150 Wing
Wing Commander R. P. Beamont
RAF No. 41800
Bradwell Bay (UK), April 1944

Ronald Thomas SUSANS DSO DFC

North American P-51D-25-NT A68-724
No. *** squadron, RAAF
Squadron Leader R. T. Susans
Bofu (Japan), 1947

James Henry LACEY DFM*

Supermarine Spitfire Mk.XIV RN135
No. 17 Squadron
Squadron Leader J. H. Lacey
RAF No. 1147504
Seletar (Singapore), autumn 1945

Introducing's RAF In Combat and Bravo Bravo Aviation's collection of
highly-detailed and historically accurate, high-quality aviation prints.
For more information on available prints, please visit :

www.RAF-IN-COMBAT.com

or

BRAVO BRAVO AVIATION
BBA
HIGH QUALITY AVIATION ILLUSTRATION
www.BravoBravoAviation.com

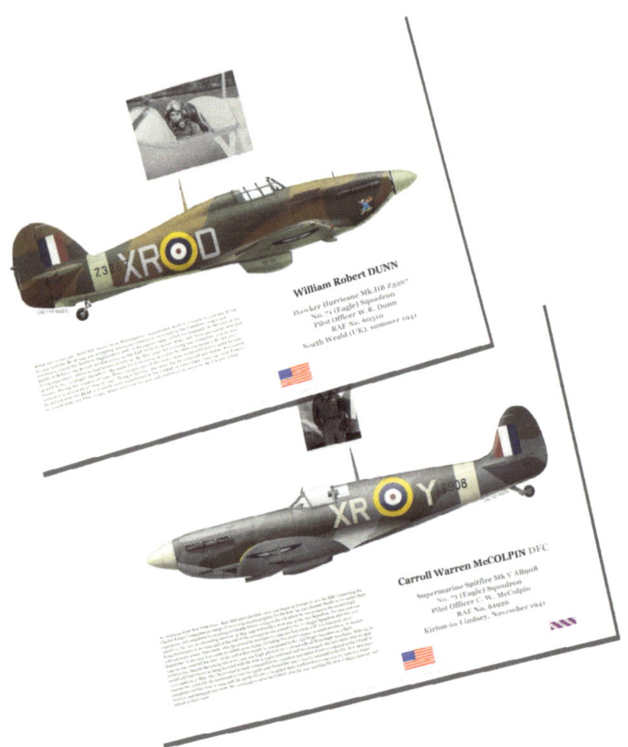

William Robert DUNN

Hawker Hurricane Mk.IIB Z3220*
No. 71 (Eagle) Squadron
Pilot Officer W. R. Dunn
RAF No. 60570
North Weald (UK), summer 1941

Carroll Warren McCOLPIN DFC

Supermarine Spitfire Mk.V AB908
No. 71 (Eagle) Squadron
Pilot Officer C. W. McColpin
RAF No. 60606
Kirton-in-Lindsey, November 1941

Prints available for this book:

PL-039: C.W. McColpin
PL-040: G.A. Brown
PL-051: D.J.M. Blakeslee
PL-055: W.R. Dunn (1)
PL-056: W.R. Dunn (2)
PL-079: E.H. Thomas (1)
PL-082: E.H. Thomas (2)
PL-185: W.M. Churchill
PL-186: W.E.G. Taylor
PL-187: S.T. Meares
PL-188: C.G. Paterson
PL-189: G.A. Daymond
PL-190: R.P.R. Powell
PL-191: H.C. Kennard
PL-192: W.D. Williams
PL-193: S.R. Edner
PL-194: J.B. Mahon